A *DOCTRINE & LIFE* SPECIAL

# No Longer Strangers

## CULTURAL INTEGRATION IN CHURCH AND SOCIETY IN IRELAND

*Edited by*

Bernard Treacy OP

*with*

Alan V. Martin *and* Tony Walsh



DOMINICAN PUBLICATIONS

First published (October 2006) by
Dominican Publications
42 Parnell Square
Dublin 1

ISBN 1-905604-05-X
978-1-905604-05-0

British Library Cataloguing in Publications Data.
A catalogue record for this book is available
from the British Library.



Cover design by Bill Bolger

Cover photograph shows
the Discovery Choir, Dublin

Printed in Ireland by
The Leinster Leader Ltd
Naas, Co. Kildare.

This work is issued to subscribers to *Doctrine & Life*
for October and November 2006
at no extra cost to their pre-paid subscriptions.

It may be cited as
*Doctrine & Life*,
vol. 55, nos. 8 and 9,
October and November 2006.

# Contents

# Contributors

**Alan V. Martin**, a minister of the Presbyterian Church in Ireland, first served in Gujarat in India. This experience enabled him and his wife to empathise with people who have left their country of birth and early influence to live and make a home in another country. On returning to Ireland, he ministered in two congregations in Co. Armagh, before spending 30 years at Abbey Presbyterian Church, in Dublin. On retiring, he gained the degree of M.Phil. at the Irish School of Ecumenics for research on which his contribution to this work is based.

**Anne Ryan** teaches in the department of adult and community education at the National University of Ireland, Maynooth, where she is also professor and head of the department.

**Bernard Treacy, O.P.**, is editor of the monthly journal *Doctrine & Life.*

**Sahr Yambasu**, whose doctorate in theology is from the University of Cambridge, taught theology at Freetown in Sierra Leone. Now an occasional lecturer at University College, Dublin, he is also Methodist minister in Galway, and chaplain at the National University of Ireland, Galway.

**Tony Whelan** is a lecturer in the department of adult and community education at the National University of Ireland, Maynooth. He is also a member of the Council on Social Responsibility of the Methodist Church in Ireland

*Erratum*

The writer described as Tony Whelan is, in fact, named Tony Walsh. Apologies to him and to readers for the confusion.

# Introduction
# Hope for a Transcultural Future

BERNARD TREACY, O.P.

The prompt for this work, *No Longer Strangers: a* Doctrine & Life *Special,* was research carried out at the Irish School of Ecumenics by Alan Martin who, when he was minister at Abbey Presbyterian Church, also on Parnell Square, was for many years a neighbour of ours at Dominican Publications. The lengthy chapter, 'The Ephesian Moment: the Possibilities of Cultural Reconciliation in a Cosmopolitan Environment', which is central to this work, presents the fruits of that research. It analyses the important factors which facilitated integration in the first Christian communities. The factors identified by sociologists were proximity, equality, authority and a sense of the common good. Christian thinking adds the elements of forgiveness and repentance as being essential to the reconciliation which can integrate people of different cultural backgrounds. 'The Ephesian Moment' also applies this analysis to the experience of Church congregations in Ireland in which there are significant numbers of immigrant members. It show, further, how proximity, equality, authority, the common good, forgiveness and repentance can together provide a template for integration within civil society also.

It is important to pay heed to the experience of people actually involved, as members or as leaders, in inter-cultural congregations, and to allow the wisdom of their experience be more widely known. To this end, a symposium was organised at the National University of Ireland, Maynooth, on 18 September 2004. This event, supported by the Irish Council of Churches and the Council on Social Responsibility of the Methodist Church in Ireland, was organised by Alan Martin and Tony Walsh. For the first time it brought together representative of some 30 culturally diverse congregations, representing a variety of denominational backgrounds. Work carried out on that day of discussion, presentation and engagement finds its way into these pages. The chapter 'Levels of Engagement between Cultures', by Anne Ryan, and Sahr Yambasu's 'Embracing the Different Other' are both based on addresses given that day. And the chapter 'Experiencing Transculturalism' introduces the experience of people present in Maynooth as well as of others involved in culturally diverse Christian communities.

It is noticeable that the great majority of the voices telling of their experiences in inter-cultural congregations come from minority Christian traditions. This may be because many immigrant Christians themselves belong to such traditions. It may also be related to the fact that evangelical Churches already experience a degree of internal diversity and that their structures are flexible, with an emphasis on the recognition and development of local leadership.

This is not to say that the Catholic and Anglican traditions are unable to form and nurture transculturalism in Church life. But the approach may be somewhat different. Representatives of Catholic parishes attended the Maynooth symposium, and were able to report on how members of immigrant communities were welcomed and were entrusted with ministries within the parish. In many dioceses and religious orders in Ireland, Polish priests have been authorised to minister as chaplains to the Polish community. Priests who have served in Brazil or Nigeria minister among Brazilian and Nigerian residents. In the Church of Ireland diocese of Dublin, the Discovery programme aims at mutual cultural enrichment between the immigrant and the indigenous communities in the Church. Many Catholic dioceses sponsor similar initiatives, while at national level the Refugee Project attached to the Commission for Justice and Social Affairs of the Bishops' Conference provides research and information to facilitate local initiatives.

The document 'The Love of Christ towards Emigrants' (*Erga Migrantes Caritas Christi*), produced at the Vatican in 2004 by the Pontifical Council for the Pastoral Care of Migrants and Itinerant People, offers many rich insights into the need to respect migrants and to welcome them. It advocates the setting up of welcome centres; it calls for the provision of emergency help, where needed; and it urges that welcome extend to ensuring 'the progressive integration and self-sufficiency of the immigrant.' It advocates that forms of prayer and devotion familiar to immigrants be incorporated into parish liturgies, and it requires that pastoral workers be competent in cultural mediation.

Important as such provisions are, perhaps the most instructive element in *Erga Migrantes* is its theological stress on the experience of migration being a constituent element in the history of salvation. It can cite the experience of Abraham and of Moses, and can point both to the Exile and to the return as being moments of traumatic dislocation for the People of God. It reminds us that our Lord was himself a migrant in Egypt. And it suggests that the Catholic tradition, in particular, should treasure contact with foreigners as being 'a visible sign and an effective reminder of that universality which is a constituent element of the Catholic Church.'

It is part of the calling of the Church to live out in each generation that grace which enabled the Ephesian Church to understand that people of diverse backgrounds are 'no longer strangers but friends'. But the Church is not alone in needing to ensure that immigrants would not remain strangers. Responsibility for enabling migrants and the indigenous population to live harmoniously and productively together rests on the State and its organs of government and of persuasion. If a multicultural approach is under question because of problems arising in countries which have made it their preferred option, the opportunity may now exist to attempt something more likely to bring long-term benefits. As all the contributions in this work demonstrate, a transcultural approach can enhance life for all the cultures involved in a community. It is not a matter of trying to mix-and-match elements dear to the various traditions involved. Instead, it is a process of learning in such a way as establishes new levels of community which are inclusive and cohesive, a community of welcome and of hope.

ACKNOWLEDGEMENTS

I close this Introduction by making glad use of the opportunity it gives to acknowledge the exceptional involvement of Alan V. Martin and Tony Walsh in the preparation of this book. And I join with them in expressing particular gratitude to Narcisse Biansumba, Bill and Doreen Colvin, Yvonne Deegan, Kevin Devlin, Pat Mullen, Jean and Ed Ritchie, Anne Ryan, and Sahr Yambasu; to all the participants in the colloquium at NUI Maynooth; and to a number of other people who wished to remain anonymous – all have given generously of their time and expertise.

# The Trauma of Cultural Displacement

TONY WALSH

It is important to address the multi-faceted nature of the trauma of displacement and the challenges of rebuilding life in a foreign culture if we are to gain insights into the processes involved in building culturally diverse community.

## DISPLACEMENT

Traumatic events call into question basic human relationships. They breach the attachments of family, friendship, love and community. They shatter the construction of the self that is formed and sustained in relation to others. They undermine the belief systems that give meaning to human experience. They violate the victim's faith in a natural or divine order and cast the victim into a state of existential crisis.

To become a refugee is to become dislocated, often separated violently from home, loved ones, work and community, and from all that is familiar and predictable. Physical, cultural, psychological and emotional displacement is at the heart of the experience.

Three distinct phases emerge as central elements of the trauma. Firstly, what is often perceived as the central axis of the experience, the actual physical uprooting, frequently takes place against a background of years of uncertainty, oppression, violence or persecution and economic deprivation, which will have taken a profound physical and emotional tole. Then comes the actual violence of physical, psychological and cultural displacement. Thirdly, this is inexorably followed not so much by the arrival in a safe haven as by the compelling necessity of engaging with an alien and often inscrutable new culture.

Such a trinity constitutes deep human trauma. It has the effect of radically disrupting the normal coping mechanisms as well as rupturing the very core of personal identity. Robert Jay Lifton, whose work on the psychological accompaniments of crisis is seminal, suggests that in a real way the survivor of such violence suffers a death: the death of the self.[1] Nothing can ever be quite the same again. What eventually may begin to emerge is a sense of survival which translates itself into the task of rebuilding identity, and the recreating of a range of relationships, and connections in which this can happen – a difficult task at the best of times but more so in a totally new world.

*Relational*

The psychological sequel of any trauma includes a sensed violation of the connection with meaningful others. And the questioning whether important human relationships are real, or of their quality. The trauma of refugee displacement adds another layer to this relational aspect.

Many refugees will have to cope with real as well as perceptual difficulties in relationship. Generally, they will, quite literally, have been torn from core relationships through removal. They may also have been forced to question existing relationships following political intrigue and subsequent betrayal in their country of origin. Some will have experienced torture at the hands of fellow nationals or even family members.

In their new context there will be difficulties as they interact with officialdom, or experience threats, rejection and negativity from existing residents. At times, there will also be the attitudes of fellow refugees to contend with as they, acting out their own saga of pain and frustration, scapegoat vulnerable newcomers and vent their anger on them. Such experiences inevitably provoke questions not only about the reliability of others, but also tend to destablise a secure sense of self, promoting internal questioning, insecurity and an undermining of confidence and appreciation of one's own value and abilities.

*Meaning*

Human beings operate within a range of accustomed belief systems which give meaning to their lives and offer generally acceptable explanations about the world and its happenings. Such belief systems offer a framework through which sense can be made of the variety of events which we encounter. Belief systems can be political, ideological or, indeed, theological. They generally encompass value systems and assump-

1. R. J. Lifton, *Death in Life: Survivors of Hiroshima*, 1991, Chapel Hill: University of North Carolina Press.

tions about how to live life, and are very connected to the values and cultures in which we live. While they vary enormously from culture to culture and from individual to individual, their function is central in creating a sense of shared order.

Trauma frequently has the result of inviting a profound questioning of these assumed values, and the world of values and belief systems rarely remains intact; it must be re-worked and re-ordered to include and make sense of both past and recent events as well as newly emergent realities.

Sudden cultural or relational displacement can also create a huge perturbation through which we recognise that our former value systems are unshared in the new context, as well as no longer functioning adequately in the task of making sense of the events of our life. For refugees, the world view developed within their home community may well need a radical re-interpretation, if not re-invention to encompass the trauma of displacement and the world of new realities, beliefs and behaviours encountered in the new cultural milieu. This constitutes the removal of another bedrock and poses the challenge of rediscovering a more useful and effective way of sense-making. Until this can happen, individuals are often cast adrift on a sea where there seem to be no certainties, no values and no certainty whatsoever.

*Resources*

The creation of a new sense of security and stability is dependant on an ability to recognise, access and utilise both internal and external resources. To be able to appreciate the internal personal resources and to recognise external resources as familiar and accessible is of prime assistance when faced with difficulty. Classical crisis theory, however, suggests that trauma results in a sense of being cut off not only from the sense of the core of self but also from one's awareness of internal resources which fuel coping mechanisms in situations of challenge. When external resources are masked by unfamiliar language, inaccessible and bureaucratic processes and difficulty of access, this add to the difficulty.

## REBUILDING

Profound as all these influences are, those who have been displaced almost without exception enter into a process of rebuilding their lives in the new context. For some, depending on their personality, their previous life experience, their level of adaptability and the level of their trauma, this will be easier than for others. There are those who will need to engage with their new world very slowly: for them the prime task may be the need for safety and security. Hence their energies will tend to go into re-creating and conserving as much as possible of the familiar. They may rarely venture outside their family, or the ethnic social or community group which they have discovered. Others will feel much more able to adventure and will have sufficient energy to engage with the new society, develop relationships and engage in creative networking.

All, however, are in a process of adaptation. Their energies for new challenges will tend to be uneven; the process of human healing is never uniform and has its own ebbs and flows. There will for years, even for those who appear strongest, be areas of huge vulnerability which, as in grief, can be brought to the surface by the most unlikely events. And people will tend to be particularly sensitive to events in the home-land and to losses or changes within the family or community of origin from whom they are now physically separated. Whether rapid or more gentle, the process of rebuilding life does have a number of particular facets.

*Re-learning*

Refugees by definition consistently find themselves in places that are culturally, linguistically and racially alien.[2] An important response is to engage in a learning project which encompasses three distinct but overlapping phases. There is the new learning that is geared towards acquiring new information. Secondly, there is the learning that is related to the development of new coping mechanisms for the new context. Finally, there is a re-viewing of one's old assumptions and ways of seeing the world.

Arrival in a new country where one is unfamiliar with the language and has little knowledge of how to access supports and no awareness of cultural norms, can pose problems for mere survival. Learning how to find accommodation, food, money, a job; how to acquire suitable clothing or even how to ascertain what clothing might be necessary in an unfamiliar climate, are all central. Focusing on how to become appraised

2. L.A. Camino and R.M. Krulfeld. 1994. 'Introduction', in L.A. Camino and R.M. Krulfeld (eds) *Reconstructing Lives, Recapturing Meaning; Refugee Identity, Gender and Cultural Change*, 1994, London: Gordon and Breach Publishers.

of one's rights, even how to discover the new norms of behaviour; how to learn a new code of behaviour and communication are among the challenges to be engaged with.

Examples of difficulty are legion. One sixteen year old African, escaping form the threat of ritual murder, arrived in Dublin alone and vulnerable on a freezing February day. He spent three nights sleeping in a phone box, because he did not know where or how to find help.

A forty year old Congolese pastor, as soon as he was able to access the basics of survival, spent as much time as possible in bed during his first six months in Ireland. Nothing in his previous life had prepared him for the cold of an Irish winter or the pain of violent separation from his wife and children; the idea of meeting and interacting with new people was too much. So he learned to coped by withdrawal. At least when he slept he could escape the pain of separation and block out the cold; so he learned to deal with the first phase of engagement in the new context.

Even when the necessities of survival are attended to, the larger and longer term questions of how to grasp the cultural norms, values and expectations of the host culture remain. Learning how to engage with the obliqueness of a strange culture, with its hidden meanings, implicit norms and unclear expectations is a huge challenge. Learning to respond appropriately is even more challenging. There are few easy ways of engaging with such subtle layers of complexity.

And then there is the subtler level of re-learning one's view of the world or the self. Sahr Yambasu gives a vivid example his own experience of having to re-learn at that more delicate level

> [L]ike a revelatory experience it suddenly occurred to me one day…that perhaps success in life is not necessarily about a constant upward climb … but is about how successfully one manages both the upward and downward trends, and also the curves. It was the dawn of a new way of seeing and being. It issued in a profound rethink of my circumstances in Ireland that led to the decision to engage in positive action with the hope of re-building my capacity for the society that I was now living in.[3]

3. S. Yambasu, 'Interrogating Displacement', in A. Ryan and T. Walsh (eds.), *Unsettling the Horses*, 2004, Maynooth: MACE, p. 38.

*Re-inventing self*

The demand is not just to make sense of a new culture; rather it is to do something much more radical. It is to re-invent the self in keeping with the demands, norms, messages and expectations of that culture.

This is always a complex and delicate process; but it is essential to finding a way of being that fits and brings the desired rewards of conformity with the new context. Even for privileged newcomers to any new culture, such as diplomatic personnel who may have an entrée to personal coaching, positions of influence and a ready-made community of support, a steep learning curve is always implied. For those without these facilities, and already rendered vulnerable by their dislocation from home, the project is particularly difficult. Behaviours and values seen as acceptable, even honoured, in the country of origin may result in misunderstanding, anger and rejection in the new. Learning to cope with such reactions as well as developing new behaviours seem essential to the process of adaptation and long term survival.

*Resourcefulness*

For those undertaking work with, or entering into relationship with refugees or asylum seekers, developing an understanding of the enormity of the displacement experience is important. This, however, is only part of the picture. In achieving an understanding of such circumstances it is essential not to be seduced by the disempowerment of sympathy alone. It is also vital to recognise the creativity and energy that can also be embedded in the experience. Most of those seeking refugee status have survived huge trauma; the fact that they have survived at all underlines their strength, adaptability and potential for continued growth and development. Esther Edeko, a Nigerian nun reporting on her research among a group of African refugees in Ireland, emphasises the profound resourcefulness which many refuges bring to bear on the huge tasks with which they are faced: '[D]espite having been violently uprooted from their home, the participants in the study demonstrated capacities for innovation and survival … they manifested the vitality to create and negotiate new roles and behaviour.' [4]

4. E. Edeko, 'Wading into Uncharted Waters' in Ryan, A. and T. Walsh (eds.), *Unsettling the Horses*. 2004, Maynooth: MACE, p. 49.

The challenge for refugees, then, is to engage in a process of recreating the self in a way that fits with the new society, with a view to creating personal stability and economic and social security. An essential part of this endeavour is to draw on the internal resources and potentials created by their whole life experience, and the resources and supports that can be marshalled within their new environment. The ability to analyse and critically reflect on both old and new cultures as well as on previous life experience are important in developing ways of responding to and managing the fresh context. The availability of support groups from the country of origin, or a community of long term residents, or a mixture of both, willing to provide a safe context in which to learn, question, experiment and explore such areas, is of huge importance in this process.

# Levels of Engagement between Cultures [1]

ANNE RYAN

Many Church congregations, whose membership is increasingly culturally diverse, are grappling with decisions about how to create an environment that facilitates interaction between people from different cultural backgrounds. These congregations are at the forefront of shaping a new era, not only in their local Church community, but also in Irish society where models of cultural inclusiveness are scarce.

Being at the forefront of any new venture is always exciting, but rarely comfortable. Breakers of new ground can find themselves isolated in systems that place little value on their endeavours. In addition they often face resistance from those who cherish established ways of doing things (not primarily because they are effective but because they are established) and who fear that disturbing the status quo will result in a loss of control. With these difficulties in mind, this chapter is intended to stimulate discussion among those who are carving a new future for their entire congregation. What follows are ideas and examples drawn from lessons that have been learned in the creation of inclusive communities. They are not meant to be prescriptive solutions to the particular difficulties and opportunities these congregations encounter. Instead, it is hoped that they will make it possible to look afresh at everyday experiences of cross-cultural interaction in ways that allow for new insights.

## RESPONDING TO CHANGE

> If one feature in our society appears to hold constant, it is the certainty of change.[2]

1. This chapter draws on a paper jointly delivered by the author and Dr Tom Collins, Director of the Dundalk Institute for Technology, at a colloquium on interculturalism at NUI Maynooth, 18th September 2004.

2. S.D. Brookfield, *Developing Critical Thinkers: Challenging Adults to Explore Alternative Ways of Thinking and Acting*, 1997, Milton Keynes: Open University Press.

There was a time in Ireland, not so long ago, when talk of population change focused on the movement of people outwards in search of employment. We talked of loss. We were preoccupied with brain drain and the problems faced by towns and villages where there were no young adults. Those days are gone. Emigration has now given way to immigration. We are experiencing the dawn of a new age of cultural pluralism. In response to these changing times, this chapter looks at how groups and 'individuals can be transformed through a process of critical reflection that involves becoming more open to the perspectives of others: being less defensive and more accepting of new ideas'.[3]

Sahr Yambasu eloquently depicts this type of *transformation* in a recent publication where he critically reflects on the series of life-changing events that caused him to journey from Sierra Leone to Ireland. Confronted by enormous change in his circumstances and in his sense of self he describes his experience as not being 'one of discovering who I am, but of creating who I want to be amidst ruptures and continuity.[4] In this statement Yambasu makes it clear that he had the power to decide who *he* wanted to be. His choice was about finding a new identity that took account of all of his past experience and let him decide how to now approach his present circumstances. His awareness of the evolving, rather than fixed, nature of identity is a truth we all need to recognise.

> Cultural ...identity is a matter of 'becoming' as well as of 'being'. It belongs to the future as well as the past. It is not something which already exists, transcending place, time, history and culture. Cultural identities come from somewhere, have histories. But, like everything which is historical, they undergo constant transformation. Far from being eternally fixed in some essentialised past, they are subject to the continuous 'play' of history, culture and power.[5]

Once we accept that identity is not a fixed end state, we realise that all of us are responsible for the role we decide to play in shaping the chang-

3. E. Edeko, 'Wading into Uncharted Waters', in A. Ryan, A. and T. Walsh, (eds), *Unsettling the Horses.* 2004, Maynooth: MACE, pp. 48-59.

4. S. Yambasu, 'Interrogating Displacement', in A. Ryan and T. Walsh, (eds), *Unsettling the Horses,* 2004, Maynooth: MACE, pp. 34-46.

5. This quotation is cited in S. Yambasu, 'Interrogating Displacement' in A. Ryan and T. Walsh (eds) *Unsettling the Horses,* 2004, Maynooth: MACE, pp. 34-46 (p. 45).

ing world in which we live. We can choose to be active players like Yambasu, or we can choose to be passive players. But there are no bystanders. Whichever way we live our lives is a decision about who we want to be and how we want to position ourselves in relation to others. We cannot escape responsibility for that decision. If we are silent and not engaged in the discussions around us – that constitutes a decision to withdraw and like all decisions it has consequences and repercussions.

Just as individuals are responsible for choosing how they want to respond to others, so too are communities and congregations responsible for the quality of the relationships that exist between members from different ethnic groups.

## MODELS OF RELATIONSHIP

A great deal has been written about how people from different cultural backgrounds relate to each other. The table on the following page gives a brief summary of four different approaches to managing cultural differences. The table is followed by a brief discussion on the salient features of each approach and the complex and mostly hidden factors that influence the way we relate. Categorising the approaches in this way can make it easier for us to reflect on how we choose to relate to others. Few communities or individuals operate exclusively within any one model. Most of us draw on all four at different times, depending on the situation. The models are not intended to deny this reality but instead are intended to give us an opportunity to become an observer of our everyday behaviour.

An *integration or assimilation* approach seeks to eliminate differences. This is generally done by supporting or forcing minority cultures to abandon their ways and adopt the culture of the dominant group. Dominance is not necessarily the prerogative of the numerically largest group; it generally accrues to the most powerful. Inherent in this approach are a narrow definition of what is acceptable and an intolerance of difference as an indication of deficiency or deviance. The dominant group see themselves as not just different but as superior or better people.[6] History is littered with examples of how groups were forced to assimilate and the

6. N. Elias, cited in T. Inglis, 'Racism, Power and Fear of Outsiders' in *The Adult Learner*, 2001, Dublin: AONTAS, pp. 7-14.

**APPROACHES TO ENGAGEMENT BETWEEN CULTURES**

| APPROACH | PRIMARY AIM | WEAKNESS |
|---|---|---|
| Assimilation | Eliminate differences through absorbtion | Domination on part of the most powerful grouping. Less powerful has to 'fit in'. |
| Multi-culturalism | Retain distinct identities | May be little communication between cultures |
| Inter-culturalism | Retain distinct identities and promote understanding between cultures | Exchanges between cultures can remain at superficial levels |
| Trans-culturalism | Promote interaction that leads to change in each culture in ways that enhance all the cultures involved | Difficult to achieve. Calls for openness in communications, constant effort and risk-taking |

efforts some made to resist the pressure and retain their way of life.[7] This is an approach that has little to offer to a community or congregation that wants to explore a more inclusive alternative. However, it is a position most likely to be evoked by those who have not questioned their own cultural beliefs, especially when they are confronted by incidents or behaviours that they are at a loss to understand within their particular cultural norms.

*Multiculturalism* acknowledges the importance of difference and the need for people to be allowed to take pride in their cultural inheritance. In practice it often leads to parallel development with little or no inter-

7. Examples of assimilation can be found in the writings of Franz Fanon who captures the psychological devastation induced by the colonisation of cultures. The policy of assimilation adopted in relation to Aboriginal peoples in Australia is well portrayed in the film *Rabbit Proof Fence.*

action between cultures. Weak links across cultures limit the potential for communication, which in turn means that the bonds of reciprocity that are an essential feature of an active community, are fragile or may even be non-existent. Interaction can be threatening for those who belong to minority groups and fear being overwhelmed by the dominant culture. This level of separateness obscures subtle but significant differences within each of the culture groups. Thus, the complexity and richness of perspective within each cultural grouping is hidden from and lost to the wider congregation. Tightly bounded separate groupings militate against developing a dynamic congregation. Instead, the congregation may be reduced to a gathering of people or a passive audience connected only by their attendance at the same place of worship.

*Interculturalism* goes beyond multiculturalism by recognising the importance of retaining distinct identities while also seeking to promote greater understanding between different cultures. Exchanges between cultures can, however, remain at functional levels such as attending the same schools and churches, utilising the same health services or working in the same place; or they may involve more direct interaction such as enjoying each others' music, food, literature. While these exchanges are important in their own right, they are not in themselves adequate to build the level of trust and the depth of understanding that enables people to be active partners in shaping their joint world.

*Transculturalism* is used here to describe a process of engagement between cultures. It is an attempt to capture the dynamic nature of such exchanges. It proposes going beyond a 'them' and 'us' divide in order to create new identities for all involved. It is not about the assimilation of one culture within another and it is not about creating a hybrid culture that is identical for all. It is about creating the conditions that allow all involved to position themselves in ways that make it possible to enter into a process that allows for understanding and change. Encounters of this nature involve on-going learning:

- learning how to engage;
- learning to take account of those factors that inhibit interactions; and
- learning to overcoming these obstacles.

Transculturalism is, therefore, about establishing and sustaining a community that is inclusive and cohesive.

### RELATING TO OTHERS

There is no blueprint for creating an inclusive community where members of every cultural grouping can take part in the life of the community and interact with each other. However, it is possible to describe those attributes or characteristic that are essential to enable such communities to emerge. Where communities have sought to create change, or to respond to change that has come upon them, the quality of the relationship between the different interest groups, and within each of the groups, is the single most important factor that determines how successful they will be.

As any group forms, or reforms to accommodate new members, it goes through cycles of ease and difficulty. Curiosity, tolerance, fear and hostility take precedence at different times. What makes for a good relationship is the willingness and capacity of groups and individuals to communicate with each other.

Good communication processes allow trust to be established. These processes may not prevent difficulties from arising; but they ensure that when difficulties do arise, they can be resolved in ways that strengthen rather than fracture the relationship. The test is whether people can talk openly about problems that emerge or whether they hide away and avoid the subject; when people do talk, a further test is whether this leads to individuals or groups getting 'blamed', resulting in them withdrawing from further engagement, or whether they feel the discussion has empowered them to re-engage. Inclusive communities are able to discuss problems. They see difficulties as opportunities to learn how to do things differently. For this to be possible, all the members have to be able and willing to participate in the community.

### PARTICIPATION

Participation is a much-used term, and how it is interpreted can vary considerably. At one end of the spectrum it means consulting with people in order to mobilise support for decisions that have already been taken by a small number of people. Where participation is limited in this way, there is no imperative towards empowerment. Those who are not party to determining priorities and setting agendas cannot influence the direction of their community and are consequently unlikely to be able to sustain commitment to the on-going long-term process of building trust. Over time those who are excluded from decisions lose interest and their level of involvement gets less and less. Eventually they confine themselves to complying with or, in some cases, resisting decisions.

At the opposite end of the spectrum, participation means involving people at every stage of decision-making; in this, its deepest manifestation, participation is seen as a mechanism for redistributing power that might otherwise be vested in a small number of people. This raises the question: 'Does everyone have to be involved in every decision?' The answer has to be 'No'. This would be impractical in a large community. However, as a general principle it is important that all those affected by a problem have a say in naming the problem and in agreeing a resolution. This kind of participatory approach takes more time than a more traditional decision-making structure but it generates the sense of ownership and commitment that is vital to build a cohesive community or congregation.

### INCLUSIVENESS

The vibrancy of a community is largely determined by the extent to which all those who belong to it feel that they have a voice. Communities are made up of individuals, not all of whom necessarily share the same dreams and aspirations. Individual differences can get blurred or negated by other more obvious similarities such as ethnicity. Nevertheless, differences due to gender, age, personality and background exist even within sub-groups that appear to be cohesive.

In community development it is common for people from the same locality who are sub-divided by age and gender and then asked to list the top three development priorities for their community, to come up with entirely different lists. If there is an opportunity for each group to compile an endless list, eventually items at the top of one group's list appear further down on another group's. It seems that once members of a group have listed their own priorities they begin to consider needs beyond their own immediate experience. This tendency to be most keenly aware of issues that impact directly on us, is hardly surprising. However, when we go into a new community it is easy to assume that every member of that community shares the same perspective and that the most vocal are representative of the range of interests across the entire population.

Creating an environment where silenced voices can emerge can be difficult. There is evidence that in certain circumstances communities deliberately suppress or mask internal differences. For example, when groups that perceive themselves to be different, encounter each other and fell threatened, the members of each group draw together to present a united front. Differences of opinion or perspective are glossed over. In this kind of environment, expressing a different viewpoint can be interpreted as 'letting the side down'.

## COMMUNICATION AND UNDERSTANDING

Communication that is grounded in trust allows communities to better understand each other. Understanding requires the capacity to 'read' the subtle and complex social codes that exist in all cultures. We draw on a range of codes when we communicate through language, gestures, tone of voice, demeanour. The values and deeply held convictions of a group are embedded in these codes. For example, what constitutes 'good manners' is part of the code and exists in all cultures. If we do not understand the code of manners in another person's culture and if they are not adhering to rules of our code, we feel confused, maybe even affronted, and we generally think of the other as having 'no manners' rather than 'different manners'. If the interaction between groups and individuals is totally choreographed within the strictures of one culture's good manners, it is difficult to have meaningful discussions.

In order to get to know each other we have to appreciate each other's values. This means getting to know the codes of the 'other' culture and, perhaps most importantly, it calls for identifying our own coded values and assumptions. Interrogating our own beliefs is difficult. We take them for granted so they are largely invisible to us. Generally, they are obvious to those who hold different values and assumptions. Consequently, we find that although we are often blind to our own beliefs we are capable of asking penetrating and provoking questions about the beliefs of others. When people from different cultures communicate with each other in an environment of mutual trust, each can assist the other to engage in the process of identifying the core values that underpin their beliefs. We can describe this as a mirroring process: 'We hold up our behaviour for scrutiny by others, and in their interpretation of our actions we are given a reflection, a mirroring of our own actions from an unfamiliar vantage point. This is how critical helpers function; they are mirrors who help us interpret and question our ideas and actions from a new viewpoint.'[8]

Getting to a stage where we understand the values embedded in our culture is not easy. Some would argue that it is an on-going lifetime process. If we decide to engage in the process we are opting to be active players in forging a community / congregation where cultural diversity can be cherished, celebrated, enjoyed and learned from in ways that will enrich all.

## MAKING THE FUTURE

The models of engagement between cultures discussed above may be useful to begin to debate issues to do with relationships within a congregation. The models could, for example, be used in the following ways:

1. As a diagnostic tool to identify the approach that best describes the current situation. If different groupings within the congregation undertake the task separately, it may emerge that there is no agreement about which model currently dominates. These differences of opinion in themselves provide useful insights. In considering how the different groupings should be formed in is important to allow for diversity of interest based on gender, age, etc., as well as culture;
2. As a stimulus to generate discussion on the 'why' questions that reveal the rationale, or the perceived rationale, for current practices and behaviours;
3. As an opportunity to ask 'what do we want to change?' 'why?' and 'what do we not want to change?', 'why?'
4. As a planning aid to decide where the congregation would like to be in the future;
5. As a prompt to discuss the 'how' questions, such as 'how will we get from where we are to where we want to be?' In answering this question the congregation is beginning to outline its vision for the future and naming the principles and values that will guide it in attaining that vision.

8. S.D. Brookfield, *Developing Critical Thinkers: Challenging Adults to Explore Alternative Ways of Thinking and Acting*, 1997, Milton Keynes: Open University Press.

# The Ephesian Moment
## The Possibilities of Cultural Reconciliation in a Cosmopolitan Environment *

ALAN V. MARTIN

> If there is one thing that social psychological theory and research have taught us about racially and ethnically diverse environments during the last forty years it is that simply putting children and young people from different backgrounds together is not enough to ensure positive social outcomes.[1]

Reconciliation is necessary if people, either individually or collectively, want to move on after a period of conflict. However, reconciliation is also needed where people live in culturally and ethnically distinct groups who may not themselves have been involved in conflict, but their ancestors were, and as a result their collective identity has developed separately. Whether it is voluntary separation or deliberate segregation, the result is often that a 'system of attitudes, actions, beliefs and structures'[2] grows within each separated group. Joseph Liechty and Cecelia Clegg describe sectarianism as such a system; but similar systems grow out of racism and other 'isms' that divide. The system can produce intolerance, bigotry, a hardening of boundaries, and in the case of a minority, hatred towards those who have a different identity.

As Joseph Liechty and Cecilia Clegg point out, such systems can continue indefinitely when the majority within each group simply 'keep colluding in low level sectarianism and subtly reinforce the divisions be-

*This chapter is based on a thesis prepared for the degree of M.Phil. at the Irish School of Ecumenics. The author is grateful to all who supported his research and study.

1. Janet W. Schofield, 'Promoting Positive Intergroup Relations in School Settings', *Toward a Common Destiny, Improving Race and Ethnic Relations in America*, eds. Willis D. Hawley and Anthony W. Jackson (San Francisco: Jossey-Bass Publishers, 1995) p. 264. Janet W. Schofield, Professor of Psychology at the University of Pittsburgh has a major research interest in social progress in desegregated schools in USA.

2. Joseph Liechty and Cecelia Clegg, *Moving Beyond Sectarianism* (Dublin: The Columba Press, 2001) p. 107.

tween groups.'[3] Initiatives therefore are needed to begin a process of reconciliation because mere proximity is not enough. The naive idea that contact between different ethnic and racial groups would automatically produce positive attitudes and behaviour changes has been rudely shattered in recent years. Positive action has to be taken to facilitate change of attitude and behaviour.

Gordon W. Allport in 1954 first suggested a multidimensional model that could provide conditions to produce positive social outcome in situations of inter-group contact. It had four conditions for success:

> The first facilitative factor is that sufficient opportunity be offered for the development of personal, satisfying interaction between people of diverse ethnic backgrounds (acquaintance potential).
>
> The second necessary requirement is for the participants in the inter-group contact to be of equal status.
>
> The third condition is that the person or institution of authority supports and validates the inter-group contact (authority norm).
>
> Finally, the fourth condition is that the nature of the contact fosters cooperation in the pursuit of common goals.[4]

I believe that, by applying this analysis to illuminate the transcultural experiment which was the early Church in the cosmopolitan cities of the Roman Empire we can throw light on the transcultural Christian congregations now found in cities and towns in the Republic of Ireland and on relations between culturally different Churches. From a theological perspective something else is needed besides these four principles. Where there has been injustice and violent conflict for prolonged periods between the groups further elements are needed – forgiveness, repentance and seeking the truth about what happened.

The cosmopolitan city creates the circumstances which, following Andrew F. Walls,[5] I call the 'Ephesian Moment'. It is a moment in history suitable for initiatives to be taken to find a deeper unity and mutual enrichment between people from various cultural backgrounds. Andrew

3. Op. cit., p. 109.

4. Gordon W. Allport, *The nature of prejudice* (New York, Doubleday/Anchor Books, 1958,) p. 205.

5. Andrew F. Walls, *The Cross-Cultural Process in Christian History* (Maryknoll, New York: Orbis Books; Edinburgh: T&T Clark, 2002) p. 72.

Walls used this expression to refer primarily to the moment in Ephesus when the Jewish and Gentile cultures came together in the early Church. This happened in other cosmopolitan cities of the Roman Empire but the significance of this transcultural experiment in Ephesus seems to have been appreciated to a greater extent than in other cities.

I wish to use this expression in a wider sense, referring to all moments in history when circumstances conspire to make possible an interaction in a deep and meaningful way of people from different cultural backgrounds. I suspect that we may have entered upon another 'Ephesian Moment'.

## 1. A Transcultural Experiment in the Cosmopolitan Cities of the Roman Empire

### CHARACTERISTICS OF ROMAN EMPIRE COSMOPOLITAN CITIES

*Towards a common culture*

Although in the villages of the Eastern Mediterranean area conservatism prevented the mixing of cultures, people who lived in the large cosmopolitan cities were moving in the direction of a common Greco-Roman culture.

This was most obvious in language. Not only was Greek spoken and understood by many but also city people used common forms in many areas of life. Inscriptions on tombs and buildings all over the East used stereotyped phrases. City councils announced decrees, clubs honoured their patrons, and people commemorated their dead in like fashion from Alexandria to Thessalonica. In each of those cities a visitor would have little difficulty recognizing the important temples, the government buildings, the agora or forum, the gymnasium and the theatre, the baths, and even the inns, caverns, and shops. To become a city dweller was to be caught up in a movement of manners, attitudes, and status that meant experiencing, to some degree, a common culture.

Greco-Roman society sought to overcome social conflict through continually extending the status of citizenship. Citizens were equal in the sight of the law. However, slaves, resident aliens and foreigners were excluded. When the Roman Empire came under threat in the third century this model of integration based on equal citizenship began to break up and people looked for other models of integration.[6]

*Mobility*

The diversity of people who inhabited these Roman cosmopolitan cities could not have been brought about without the considerable mobility that people enjoyed at that time. People could travel along the straight Roman roads between one city and another. There was an element of risk in that travellers could be robbed, and staying in a strange city required precautions; but the security of the empire and the good road system made mobility possible to a much greater extent than had previously been known.

*Homogeneous associations*

Those who settled in these cities in the Mediterranean world of the first century in the course of their work mixed with people from various cultural/ethnic backgrounds and status: free Roman citizens, Greeks, freed former slaves, slaves, trade and craftsmen. It should not be assumed that these cities were similar to industrial cities of today with large numbers of workers being pulled in to feed the industrial machine. Those privileged to live in the cities of antiquity were mostly there to serve the needs of the elite. There is also evidence that some people whose position in society gave them greater security, were prepared to socialize beyond their own family or village circle in associations of common interest. Indeed the early Roman Empire witnessed a growth of clubs, guilds, and associations of all sorts. The associations were of merchants, tradesmen and sometimes people who shared a common craft. However, it was normally people of the same social status and intellectual interests who became members of these associations.

*Collective Persons*

While these circumstances created the possibility of people meeting across cultural/social/ethnic boundaries, certain other forces still worked in the opposite direction. Newcomers in these big cities would settle in districts occupied by people from the same kith and kin. Writing about persons who lived in that period, Bruce J. Malina says:

6. Gerd Theissen, *The Social Setting of Pauline Christianity* (Edinburgh, T&T Clark, 1982) p. 109

> It is important not to consider them as individualistic. First-century Mediterranean persons were strongly group-embedded, collectivistic persons. They were most concerned with family integrity. Since they were group-oriented, they were socially minded, attuned to the values, attitudes and beliefs of their in-group. Because of their in-group enculturation, they were used to assessing themselves and others in terms of stereotypes often explained as deriving from the geographical location of a group.[7]

The characteristics of the various ethnic groups were said to derive from the places they inhabited. The air they breathed and the water they drank affected their corporate personality according to the Hippocratic *corpus*, an anthology of the writings of several authors, popularly attributed to Hippocrates. Thus there was considerable stereotyping of each ethnic group by which other groups might assess them. For example, Josephus describes the Tiberians as people who have 'a passion for war';[8] the Scythians 'delight in murdering people and are little better than wild beasts';[9] 'Cretans are always liars, evil beasts, lazy gluttons'.[10]

The ancient Mediterraneans were also prone to dividing the peoples of the world between their own broad ethnic group and the rest of the world. Greek writers in general spoke of 'Greek and Barbarian'. Paul of Tarsus would speak of 'Judean and Greek' (Rom. 1:16). The writer of Acts makes the same generalizations (Acts 14: 1).

Thus the circumstances of the first century made possible the coming together of people from diverse backgrounds but other social forces had the effect of preventing this happening to any significant extent. It would take something special to overcome these forces and create a community in which people from different cultural, religious, social and ethnic backgrounds could belong together.

## THE EARLY CHURCH AS A TRANSCULTURAL EXPERIMENT

The 'something special' was the early Church that brought together

7. Bruce J. Malina, *The Social World of Jesus and The Gospels* (London & New York, Routledge, 1996,) p. 64

8. Josephus, *Life*, p. 352 Loeb

9. Josephus, *Against Apion* p. 269 Loeb

10. Titus 1:12

Jew and Gentile, rich and poor, master and slave, men and women. The early Church grew, as is well attested in the New Testament, in Antioch, Corinth, Philippi, Ephesus and Rome. Not so well known is that the early Church also grew in Lyon and Carthage. All were cosmopolitan cities. The four elements outlined by Gordon Allport were present in the early Church. In addition, because of the Jewish/Gentile history of conflict and their sense of sin before God, they needed to have the elements of forgiveness and repentance.

*Proximity or Social Space*

In order to build up good relationships where people can feel 'at home' with one another it is necessary to create a space where people can meet. Reconciliation requires a locus, a place where people and things come together.

The actual place where this new community met was often the home of a leader, including women such as Lydia with independent means. Frequent meeting in the one place where members became part of a new family produced a strong sense of belonging. The house where they met must have been regarded as welcoming for both Jews and Gentiles and people of all strata of society. It might be described as a neutral but safe place in which such a diverse group could meet. Evidence suggests that they met frequently and often at paschal solemnities for the whole night. Tertullian called these meetings 'nocturnal convocations.'[11]

The Gentiles who became 'God-fearers' attended Jewish synagogues and became accustomed to the type of worship associated with the synagogue but they did not socialize with Jews. The cultural boundary marker for Jews was table fellowship. That was reserved only for fellow Jews. This restriction at the heart of this tentative Jewish/Gentile relationship as it developed in the cosmopolitan cities of the Roman Empire was an insurmountable obstacle. The breakthrough came with the sharing of meals by both Jews and Gentiles within the Christian community. The importance of these fellowship meals in the creation of the early Church cannot be emphasized enough.[12]

11. Tertullian, Essay *To His Wife.* as cited by Alan Kreider, *The Change of Conversion and the Origin of Christendom,* (Harrisburg, PA, Trinity Press International, 1999) p. 12

12. Philip Esler, *Community and Gospel in Luke-Acts* (Cambridge, Cambridge University Press, 1987) p. 89.

The welcoming house of a Christian leader where people of all ethnic groups and social status met and shared meals was necessary before in-depth interaction between Jew and Gentile was possible.

*Authority*

The authority recognized by all in the early Church was Jesus Christ. 'Paul tolerated those with ideas very different from his own... However a line has to be drawn somewhere and that is the primacy of Christ.'[13]

Many scholars today begin their commentaries on the Gospels by asking why the Gospel was written. They come to the conclusion that it was not just to preserve the stories of Jesus' ministry in writing but also to find authority in the life and teaching of Jesus for some of the things that were happening in the Christian community in which the author lived. The early Christians felt guided by the Spirit but the need for authority for what they were doing that came from Jesus must also have been strongly felt.

The ultimate authority of the early Church upon which they based their vision of a universal transcultural community was the reconciling work of Jesus whom they called the Christ. While the Jesus Movement began exclusively among Jews it changed, in the forties of the first century, to a movement for both Jews and Gentiles. It could not have done this without the acceptance of an authority that approved of this change. Above all, the authority of Jesus was needed to justify the incorporation of Gentiles into the Church without the requirement of first becoming Jews. Indeed they searched the Scriptures of the Old Testament to find further authority in the universal purpose of God fulfilled in Jesus Christ.

*Luke/Acts*

The author of Luke/Acts, according to Philip Esler,[14] wrote his account of the ministry of Jesus and the story of the early Church to legitimate the development of his local Christian community in a Roman cosmopolitan city, probably Antioch, into a Jewish/Gentile community. He wanted them to know that they had the authority and example of Jesus and that of the main apostles for doing so.

13. James Dunn, *Unity and Diversity in the New Testament* (London, SCM Press Ltd, 1977) p. 270

14. Esler, op. cit., p. 2.

The view taken by Philip Esler is that there were a significant number of Jews and Gentiles in Luke's community in Antioch. Most of the Gentiles had not converted to Christianity from paganism, but had previously been associated with Jewish synagogues. Esler argues, convincingly, that Luke attempts to justify the current practices and beliefs of his community made up of Jews and Gentles by finding authority for them in the ministry of Jesus and the events of the Church's first generation.

The universalist theme in Luke-Acts commences with the words of Simeon, who recognizes in Jesus the salvation which God has prepared before all peoples, 'a light for the illumination of the Gentiles and the glory of your People Israel' (Lk 2:31-2). It should be noted that Simeon also includes Israel in the divine plan. Soon after this, Luke alters Mark by extending the quotation from Isaiah 40 to include the words of Isaiah 40:5 'and all humanity will see the work of God' (Lk 3:5-6). Luke traces the genealogy of Jesus back to Adam (Lk 3:23-38).

*Mark 6:33-44 and 8:1-9*

According to Ched Myers,[15] Mark interprets two incidents in the ministry of Jesus to point to a new community that would include both Jews and Gentiles. Mark shows Jesus making a number of crossings from one side of the Sea of Galilee to the other. This is significant because from the names of people and places mentioned it becomes clear that one area is Jewish (Mk 5:21ff) and the other is Gentile (Mk 7:24ff). In the Jewish part of the country after healings Jesus feeds a crowd of Jewish people and there is food left over.

In the Gentile area known as the 'Decapolis' Jesus heals a Syro-Phoenician woman and a Gentile man who cannot speak. Then he feeds a Gentile crowd. He has compassion for them too. Again the crowd is satisfied and again there is a superabundance and food left over. Feeding the people was expected of the Messiah; but these twin feedings of Jewish and Gentile crowds point to a significant enlargement of the role of the Messiah.

Where there is conflict between two ethnic groups with a different culture and traditions, you would not expect these crowds to eat together

15. Ched Myers, *Binding the Strong Man, A Political Reading of Mark's Story of Jesus* (Maryknoll, New York, Orbis Books, 1988) p. 205.

and they do not. These two crowds gather on different sides of the Sea of Galilee and between the two feedings Mark says that Jesus and the disciples had to cross the Sea of Galilee and that the crossing was difficult. In other words a great gulf separates the two sides. Yet Jesus with his disciples – however reluctantly – deliberately travel from one side to the other so that Jesus can feed both.

They travel by *boat* and 'they have only *one loaf* with them in the *boat.*'[16] (My italics) The *boat*, down through the centuries, has been recognized as a symbol of the Church. In the boat is *one loaf*, another clue, and it is to be shared by everyone in the *boat.* Only *one loaf* is needed because separate bread will not be needed for the Jewish and non-Jewish disciples of Jesus.[17] In other words Jesus is not content to feed the Jewish and Gentile crowds separately but he seeks to form a new community of people who can eat together or show solidarity that transcends cultures and national differences. This interpretation of these events seems to justify and give authority for the coming together of Jews and Gentiles in a new community called the Church.

Many references in the Gospels to the salvation of Gentiles are probably redactional: Lk 2:32; 3:6; 4:27; Mk 8:1-10; Mt 10:18. In general, the Gospels portray Jesus as much more open in his relationships with Samaritans than were his Jewish contemporaries. The climax of all the Gospels is the resurrection of Jesus interpreted as giving God's authority to the life and work of Jesus. In other words the early Christians believed that this new transcultural community was created by God and that God would give them life-long support, encouragement and justification for participation in this new creation.

*Acts*

The Acts of the Apostles describes the birth of the Christian Church (*Ecclesia*) through the coming of the Holy Spirit.[18] Those present from many countries all hear the words of the disciples in their own tongue. In other words, the new community of the Church will bring unity without destroying diversity of language or culture. The emergence of this new cross-cultural community is then described but at every significant

16. Mark 8:14, Jerusalem Bible
17. Ched Myers, op. cit., p. 225
18. Acts 2:1-13

point it is shown to be under the authority and indeed the direct guidance of the Holy Spirit. It was not the product of a carefully worked out human plan. At each new stage in its development it is the Spirit that guides and prompts action.

The authority for members of the early Church came from what they believed to be the ultimate authority, namely God. More specifically, it was the authority of the God who, they believed, was revealed in Jesus Christ whose Spirit continued to guide them.

*Equality*

Roman citizenship conferred equality upon all granted that status. However, as we have seen, citizenship could not be conferred on slaves, resident aliens or foreigners. By contrast in the early Church membership was extended to women, foreigners and slaves. For in Christ there was 'neither Jew nor Greek ... neither slave nor free... neither male nor female, for you are all one in Christ Jesus' (Gal 3:28). In Christ there was equality yet distinctions were not destroyed.

Distinctions between Jews and Greeks were not destroyed. The early Church was not a celebration of cultural homogeneity. It was a celebration of a union between two entities, one Jewish and the other Gentile, the breaking down of the wall of partition between them brought about by Christ's death (Eph 2:13-18). Gentiles were not asked to become Jews. It was a celebration of diversity because humanity is diverse. Yet it was a celebration of being one because Christ is one. Those Ephesian Christians discovered that only together could they be complete in Christ.

Gerd Theissen describes this new community as 'Christian love-patriarchalism.'[19] There is evidence that some who joined were from wealthier classes and sometimes from positions of responsibility: Sosthenes was a Jewish synagogue leader; Aquila was a small businessman whose house was used for a congregation in Corinth; the house of Gaius served the entire Church; Lydia ran a small business. These leaders may have provided the houses and organization but they did not set themselves apart from other members of lower social status. The practice of having all things in common may have lapsed fairly soon in the early Church but they still regarded all members as essentially equal before

19. Gerd Theissen, op. cit., p. 107.

Christ. The early Church did not attempt to destroy social distinctions, e.g. between slave and free, but rather to establish a pattern of relationships of respect, concern and responsibility.

This becomes evident in the advice of Paul in his letter to the Christian community in Corinth on the matter of a division between those who eat well (including meat) at Christian gatherings and those who have plainer meals (1 Cor 11:17-34). His advice comes in verses 33 and 34, 'So then, my brothers, when you meet for the Meal, wait for each other; anyone who is hungry should eat at home. Then your meeting will not bring your condemnation.' The wealthier had started to have a 'private' meal separate from the poor.

Paul's advice seems to be a compromise in that he acknowledges that the wealthy can have their own private meal in their home if they so want, but it would obviously be more community-building to share that meal. However, the part of the meal that involves the elements of bread and wine by which the body and blood of Christ are to be received also has a social purpose. Paul writes, 'Because there is one bread, we who are many are one body.' This means that those who eat the one loaf are brought together in a unity that transcends other divisions. Here is illustrated the deep equality that binds this new community together yet also the differences of wealth that prompt the compromise suggested by Paul.

In Acts 6 there is an example of the seriousness with which a dispute about equal treatment between two cultural and linguistic groups is taken. The Greek-speaking Hellenists from the *diaspora* complain that the Aramaic-speaking Jews from Palestine are not distributing the daily food ration fairly. One can assume there were additional reasons for this quarrel. The apostles called the whole community together to choose seven men of good standing to 'wait on tables'. From the names of the seven we can see that all were Hellenists. Representatives of the injured party were asked to take care of all the widows.

These two incidents illustrate that while equality was never easy to maintain in practice, the early Church did make strenuous efforts to treat members fairly.

*Common Goal*

Amongst the early Christians there seems to have been a common goal of being a distinctive people, practicing values different from society as a whole.[20]

Their Christian lifestyle was partly the result of their self-identity as 'resident aliens.'[21] They were members of a community that spanned the Roman Empire yet transcended it. Christian congregations expressed this reality by corresponding with other Churches, by providing hospitality to travellers, who seemed to be numerous, and by supporting other Christians who were prisoners doing service in the mines. They empowered the weak, including an unusual freedom to women to do significant things. They engaged in economic sharing amongst the local members of house Churches. When held separately from the Eucharist the *agape* meals became an instrument for this sharing among themselves.

The sharing reached beyond the local Christian community. In 1 Corinthians 16:1ff Paul organizes a collection to be taken up amongst the Christians in Corinth for the poorer Christians in Jerusalem. A detail reveals how Paul strove to make people feel responsible for their actions in taking up the collection and not just because he asked them to do it. In verse 3 he writes, 'I will send to Jerusalem with letters of introduction those people *you approve* to deliver your gift' (my italics). They were to choose those who would bear the gift to Jerusalem.

Nor did they restrict their charitable works to members of the Church; they also helped those in need in their locality.[22] A fascinating example comes from early fourth-century Egypt, where press gangs were abducting peasants and shipping them down the Nile for service in the Roman legions. In Thebes the Christian Church heard of conscripts in their local jail; the military authorities had put them there to prevent them from escaping before they transported them further. When the Christians heard that the prisoners were in distress, they brought them food, drink, and other necessities. One of the conscripts, Pachomius, asked what was going on. The people coming to his aid, he was told, were Christians who 'are merciful to everyone, including strangers.' Pachomius had never heard of Christians, so he asked for more information: 'They are people who bear the name of Christ, the only begotten Son of God, and

20. Wayne A. Meeks, *The First Urban Christians* (New York & London, Yale University Press, 1983) p. 89.

21. Alan Kreider, *The Change of Conversion and the Origin of Christendom* (Harrisburg, PA, Trinity Press International, 1999) p. 15.

22. Kreider, op. cit., p. 19.

they do good to everyone, putting their hope in Him who made the heaven and earth and us humans.'[23]

Inspired by the Christians' visit and material aid, Pachomius prayed to God to deliver him, promising that if he was delivered he would serve God all his days. Shortly afterwards he was discharged and after being instructed was baptized. It was the attractive charitable behaviour of the Christians that caused Pachomius to become a Christian.

These charitable acts were not just the spontaneous acts of individuals but a deliberate policy in which every new member of the community had an apprenticeship before admission to baptism. Documents reveal that catechumens [24] were asked to make life-long commitment to charitable work both within their congregation and amongst the poor outside the Christian community. There seems little doubt that so much activity towards a common goal strengthened their sense of being together in a great enterprise.

*Additional Elements of Reconciliation: Forgiveness and Repentance*

The four principles or elements propounded by Gordon Allport for creating good interaction between people from different cultures illuminate what happened in the early Church. They helped to produce the dynamics of reconciliation within the Church. Yet it is also true that the distinctively Christian elements of forgiveness and repentance were needed to produce the deeper and long-lasting reconciliation that was needed to overcome antagonism that had been passed from one generation to another.

The early Church must have had some members who from their collective past bore resentment against others in the Church. Yet the writer of the Letter to the Ephesians can say that through Christ both Jews and Gentiles are one: 'So you are no longer aliens or foreign visitors; you are fellow citizens with the holy people of God…' (Eph 2:19). Both a letting go of the past (forgiveness) and a change of attitude (repentance) are implied.

It is constantly stated that the early Christians believed that it was through Jesus that forgiveness of sins was proclaimed to them. (Acts 13:38)

23. First Greek Life of Pachomius 4-5 as cited by Alan Kreider, op., cit., p. 19.
24. Kreider, pp. 4-5.

The call then to practise forgiving others rests upon first receiving it. As it is put in Ephesians 4:32, 'Be generous to one another, sympathetic, forgiving each other as readily as God forgave you in Christ.' This grace of forgiveness was constantly proclaimed to them through baptism and the Lord's Supper. The celebration of the Eucharist makes real to participants that they are invited in and accepted; but they are then expected to become agents of the same forgiveness and acceptance. They are expected to change their attitudes and repent. As Miroslav Volf puts it, 'What happens to us must be done by us.'[25] This is why those participating in the Eucharist exchanged the sign of peace.

*Settling Disputes*

Though the history of the Church shows many failures to practise forgiveness and repentance and actively engage in conflict resolution, the early Church did actually practice settling disputes using the authority of Jesus.

Paul had strong words to offer on disputes within the Church. Despite the diversity of members, the Church is one body in Christ, he writes (1 Cor 12). Disputes within the Church threaten unity in Christ he asserts, thus weakening the primary evidence of Christ's saving power.

Paul is not so much concerned about the existence of the disputes among Christians as he is with how disputes are resolved. He makes requests for the appointment of mediators, 'yokefellows' as he calls them (Phil 4:2-3). A similar pattern appears in 1 Corinthians 6:1-7, where Paul is scathing about Christians taking disputes to secular courts instead of resolving them with the help of Christian mediators: 'How dare you go to law before the unrighteous instead of the saints?'[26] The Church is to provide a forum for resolving disputes within the fellowship of believers.

Paul is here developing the teaching already familiar from the tradition of Jesus who placed the settlement of disputes at the heart of how the Church should function. Jesus called the process 'binding and loosing' (Mt 18:15-20). This was the phrase he used for the exercise of Church authority (Mt 16:13-20), and he stated that it had eternal significance.

There is a reference to settling disputes in Matthew 18, though it is

25. Miroslav Volf, *Exclusion and Embrace*, p. 129.
26. 1 Cor 6:5

not often seen as such. In verse 20, Jesus promised that, 'Wherever two or three are gathered together in my name there am I in the midst of them.' Modern readers usually take this as a mandate for a small prayer meeting. However, examination of the context leaves no room for this interpretation. The whole chapter is focused on relationships and misunderstandings and this verse is clearly linked to that theme. Moreover, 'two or three gathered' is a phrase familiar from Old Testament usage. In the context of adjudicating disputes it indicates an acceptable quorum of witnesses (Deut 17:6; 19:15; Heb 10:28). Thus it seems clear that Jesus' words are intended for peace-making. Where believers gather to resolve disputes in his name, Christ is present among them.

The resolution of disputes in this way stood out in contrast to the use of violence in the Roman Empire. To be consistent those who became members of the Church had not only to practise the resolution of disputes within the Christian community but also to refuse to conform to the generally accepted behaviour of that time. Thus the early Church for about 300 years forbade all Christians from taking part in war. Christian authors, such as Clement of Alexandria, Justin Martyr from Greece, Tertullian from North Africa, all writing between the years 150 and 250, reflected the view that Christians should not take part in war, a view that seems to have characterized the Church then. At about the same time, Origen, who lived in Egypt and Palestine, expressed his understanding of this vision in the following words:

> And to those who inquire of us whence we come, or who is our founder, we reply that we are come, agreeably from the counsels of Jesus, to 'cut down our hostile and insolent "wordy" swords into ploughshares, and to convert into pruning hooks the spears formerly employed in war.' For we no longer take up 'sword against nation.' Nor do we 'learn war any more,' having become children of peace, for the sake of Jesus, who is our leader.[27]

In summary, Paul's attention to disputes, and the strength of his words on this topic arise from a source deeper than the concern that any leader would naturally have for harmony within the flock. Paul understood that

27. Cyril C. Richardson, ed., *Early Christian Fathers*, The Library of Christian Classics, vol. 4, (Philadelphia: Westminster Press, 1953) p. 558.

Christ came to reconcile. Reconciliation is the primary mark of redemption. The Church, Paul asserts, must take responsibility for inviting new believers, not only to do good works, but to participate in the concrete tasks of reconciliation that are the primary manifestation of God's new community.

*Completion*

Those early Christians also looked forward. They realized that what they were experiencing was a foretaste, a sign that the completion of all things in Christ will come when all the cultures of the world find oneness in him.

The completion of the Ephesian moment will be when all the cultural segments in the world become inter-active in one body. Realizing the power of Christ to break down walls of division in their new community they were filled with hope that this same power would bring all things together. It was a present experience but also a goal towards which God was moving. It was something that had happened yet was still to be completed. Duncan Forrester puts it this way: 'When we speak of reconciliation, as Christians we see it as a gift, a promise and a hope on the basis of the reconciliation which has already been achieved.'[28]

## 2. The Experience of Contemporary Transcultural Congregations, and Church Relations in the Republic of Ireland

CHARACTERISTICS OF IRISH COSMOPOLITAN URBAN AREAS.

Irish urban society has been until the 1990s fairly homogeneous. People wanted to know from where you came. When they found an answer they were satisfied that in some way they knew who you were. But in the towns and cities of the Republic of Ireland today there is a mixture of cultures, people from various countries in Eastern Europe, Asia and Africa. In addition, there are more and more Irish people finding work in and settling in the cities, leaving farming or returning from abroad. Eng-

28. Duncan B. Forrester, 'Politics and Reconciliation,' *Reconciliation in Religion and Society*, ed. Michael Hurley (Belfast, Institute of Irish Studies 1994) p. 117.

lish is the common language for this mix of people and a common consumer and freedom-loving culture pervades all groups. TV soaps, sport and the problems of congestion on the roads and finding housing all provide common points of interest. The straight Roman roads provided the means for mobility in the Roman Empire. Today it is cheap airlines and communications that enable relatives to communicate quickly.

Cities in the USA, Europe and Australia are cosmopolitan places to an extent that is greater than in previous centuries. One in three of the residents of an average European city today are immigrants. Indeed it may be necessary to go back to the cosmopolitan cities of the Roman Empire to find comparable diversity.

Yet the stereotyping of one group by another that was a characteristic of ancient Mediterranean society has its parallels in Irish society today. There are some forces working against the full integration of new residents in Irish society.

*Racism*

According to an international declaration on race and racial pride,

> Any theory which involves the claim that racial or ethnic groups are inherently superior or inferior, thus implying that some would be entitled to dominate or eliminate others, presumed to be inferior, or which bases value judgements on racial differentiation, has no scientific foundation and is contrary to the moral and ethical principles of humanity.[29]

Racism was created in the context of colonialism. Robbie McVeigh and Ronit Lentin state: 'In the act of defining African as "black" and "savage" and excluding them from their world, Europeans in the eighteenth and nineteenth centuries represented themselves as "white" and "civilized".'[30]

In a country that did not have an empire like other European countries and from which many of its citizens emigrated to find work in England, USA and Australia, it is strange that racism should be a problem. One possible explanation is given by Bill Rolston and Michael Shannon

29. UNESCO 1978, article 2:1,

30. Robbie McVeigh and Ronit Lentin, *Racism and Anti-Racism in Ireland* (Belfast: Beyond the Pale Publications Ltd., 2002) p. 1.

who point out that

> By 1830 Irish men constituted 42 percent of the British Army at a point when the Irish made up 32 per cent of the United Kingdom population overall. That disproportionate representation persisted even after the devastation of the Famine on the Irish population; in 1881 21 per cent of the British Army was Irish while 15 per cent of the United Kingdom population was Irish. Twelve per cent of naval officers between 1793 and 1815 were Irish, as were one quarter of the seamen with Nelson at Trafalgar. In the early 1880s 30 per cent of surgeons in the British Army were Irish.[31]

Irish people played a large part in the military history of the British Empire. In India, William Henry Tone, brother of Wolfe Tone, was a colonel in the service of an Indian ruler and died in battle. John Lawrence from Derry was at the forefront of the suppression of the Indian Mutiny in 1857. Brigadier-General Reginald Dyer (born in India of an Irish father and educated in Cork) opened fire without warning on an unarmed crowd in Amritsar resulting in 379 people dead and 1,200 injured.

For the Catholic working class, service to the British Empire, especially in the army, was a way out of poverty: 'The Irish soldier among Britain's 'regulars', then, was typically a Catholic, but a Catholic of low income, poorer than those who took up arms against Britain [in Ireland] from time to time and poorer than those who did not serve.'[32]

Irish involvement was not confined to the British Army, however. In 1857, when Ireland's population was 30% of that of the United Kingdom, Irish universities supplied 33% of Indian Civil Service recruits. In the 1890s, Irish men governed seven of the eight provinces of India. So Ireland's contribution to the British Raj was out of all proportion to her size. Nor was this conclusion confined to India: Irishmen played key administrative and military roles throughout the British Empire at its height.

Thus tens of thousands of Irish people encountered racially and cul-

31. Bill Rolston and Michael Shannon, *Encounters – How Racism Came to Ireland* (Belfast: Beyond the Pale, 2002) p. 56.

32. Peter Kartsten, 'Irish Soldiers in the British Army, 1792-1922: Suborned or Subordinate?', *Journal of Social History* XVII (1983) p. 37.

turally different people from the perspective of a foreign army or administration. Such was their involvement in the empire that not many made common cause with these people. On the contrary, they were likely to return to Ireland with tales of heroic conquests and massacres and thus pass on racist views to others who had never met people who were different.

The Irish missionary movement, involving as it did large numbers of people, both Catholic and Protestant, also shares some responsibility in passing on racist views. At its height in the eighteenth and nineteenth centuries missionary activity involved one in every 120 Irish adults. While abroad, many missionaries built close relations with those amongst whom they worked, but the stories that needed to be told back home to raise money to support such a massive enterprise often gave the impression that those working on the mission field were dealing with inferior people. It tended to produce patronizing attitudes amongst those who remained in Ireland but supported the work. Appeals were made for financial support for helping the orphan, hungry and destitute but seldom were questions asked as to why people were in such a condition.

This sometimes forgotten history may partly explain how racism is quite so strong in Ireland. It is certainly one of the forces against which transcultural congregations in Ireland must strive.

## TRANSCULTURAL CONGREGATIONS IN IRELAND

The focus of this study and of the survey I undertook of transcultural congregations in Ireland has been upon the admittedly small but significant number of congregations that have used the new cosmopolitan circumstances to experience a much deeper fellowship that crosses cultural boundaries. There are about 30 transcultural congregations and Christian fellowships in the Republic of Ireland. I define these as having at least 25% of total membership from new immigrants. Each has welcomed significant numbers of new residents into their fellowship or in the case of a few migrant congregations welcomed old residents.

Compared with other countries in Europe the number of transcultural congregations in Ireland is above average. Throughout Europe the established or predominant Church has often been unable to receive members with a different cultural and confessional background.

In Norway the Lutheran Church is the established Church with 86% of the population as members, yet only a relatively small number of new immigrants have joined. The Catholic Church there, on the other hand, has become a transcultural Church. In Germany there are only a small number of transcultural congregations. In Holland the Moluccan Christians, who came from former colonies from 1951 onwards, 'received very little attention from the established Churches on their arrival.'[33] These were mostly Reformed Churches. In England the first wave of immigrants in the 1950s who came from the Caribbean, were not welcomed to the extent they should have been by the established Church. There are now a number of transcultural congregations mostly in the South of England. In Ireland the pattern has been similar. It is the smaller Churches in the Republic of Ireland that seem to have been more successful in welcoming members from different backgrounds.

*Proximity*

Members of transcultural congregations meet frequently together in the same building. Social space is of course more than a physical space. It is a *locus* where people meet, talk, interact, share and learn about each other. This happens in the transcultural congregations through common worship, shared meals – often to celebrate an event such as a naming ceremony, a Baptism – or in Bible study and prayer meetings, excursions and conversations over tea/coffee. The depth of the interaction varies from congregation to congregation and between individuals but usually develops after initial awkwardness in speaking to people who are different has been overcome.

The opportunity for people from varied backgrounds to meet and interact depends to a great extent on the amount of time that members of a transcultural congregation are prepared to spend together. The depth of the interaction is greatly curtailed if it only happens once a week for one hour. Tony, a leader in a Dublin Methodist Church, a transcultural congregation, says,[34] 'It is very important to spend time in conversation, sharing experiences, getting to know each other.'

33. J.M. van Kruis, 'The 'Multi-cultural' Society and the Churches in the Netherlands,' *Culture Divides – the Gospel Unites?* (Brussels: The Churches' Commission for Migrants in Europe, 2002) p. 71.

34. This and subsequent quotations from Tony Walsh and Narcisse Biansumba come from my interviews broadcast on Sunday 2 March 2003 on RTÉ (radio).

Good leadership can help to furnish buildings in such a way that they clearly indicate a welcome to people from various nationalities and cultures. This in turn encourages the process of integration. Fr Philip Sumner, a Catholic priest in Oldham with 24 years experience of working in a transcultural parish in Mosside, Manchester, lays great emphasis on symbols that are immediately obvious on entry into the Church building used by such a congregation. He requests from every cultural group attending his Church that they prepare a Christian symbol large enough to be easily seen. It can be a banner, picture or other object that represents their culture. In this way it is made clear to anyone who enters that this place welcomes and values 'my' cultural group.

*Equality*

Christians from overseas and Irish Christians who decide to worship together will certainly face many difficulties; but most who do so, say that although the challenges are great the fruits are very precious. They see the importance and significance of becoming part of a transcultural congregation in Ireland. Some maintain a membership of both a transcultural congregation and a migrant congregation.

One of the challenges to be faced is how to provide a fair balance between the various cultures and sometimes languages of those represented. There is a need to find a balance of both styles of worship and culture in the common worship. Participation and input need to be encouraged from all. Whether it be through informal or more formal styles of worship there is need for careful planning to ensure that one cultural group does not get privilege or become dominant. In the Roman Catholic Church in Oldham, Lancashire, England, the priest encourages each cultural group to find a representative who is prepared to be trained to read the Scriptures, act as a cantor or become a minister of the Eucharist. This ensures that the congregation witnesses a balanced participation of the different cultures at Mass. In the Catholic parish church in the centre of Tralee, Co. Kerry, a similar plan operates with a reader from Nigeria, a cantor from the Philippines and a minister of the Eucharist from Zimbabwe.

In Churches where the style of worship is less formal members are encouraged to take part but in order to ensure that this results in a balanced representation some planning is necessary. Tony, a leader in a

Dublin Methodist Church where the style of worship is informal, says:

> The worship is both informal and participative but strangely both these aspects have to be well planned in order to work properly. The planning needs to involve leaders from all the cultural groups who therefore have to respect and recognize the leadership of each other. This recognition is at a lower level than official recognition of ministries between two or more Churches but it is nevertheless very important. Open times of prayer are a feature at our weekly worship. People feel free to pray aloud in 4 or 5 different languages – English, French, Portuguese and Lingala.

Narcisse, a leader in a Dublin Methodist Church, and from Congo, says, 'God has no special language. God understands all languages. It is good that our Irish brothers and sisters to hear us praying to God in our own language.'

In a congregation in Galway an African musical group regularly lead the praise for a period of 15 minutes. The decibels from the drumbeats have been reduced by agreement so as to be acceptable to European ears. If they so wish, people may pray aloud simultaneously in any language during the prayers of intercession under the guidance of a leader. This is all very different to the style of worship practiced in that congregation before the influx of new residents; yet a fair balance of cultures and style seems to have been reached and is acceptable to all. This does not happen without patient discussion and willingness to give and take.

Sometimes in such local Churches there can be considerable differences in the financial position between an established Irish member and a new immigrant. The giving of monitory gifts to those less well off must be done with great care. Paternalism, jealousy and suspicion of unequal treatment can easily arise.

*Authority*

In transcultural congregations it is evident that all accept the authority of Jesus Christ. In the survey I asked if there was serious disagreement on points of doctrine. The answers revealed that there was little and that all accepted Jesus Christ as Lord and Saviour. More specifically, they acknowledged that in committing themselves to membership of a transcultural congregation they were following the teaching of Jesus and the example of the early Church. Many also acknowledged the leading of the Holy Spirit. Narcisse, a leader in a Dublin Methodist Church said, 'There was no meeting to decide to set up a transcultural Church. It was the work of the Spirit that brought us together.' Tony added, 'Yes. The work of the Spirit is a process of development, change, growth and challenge.'

Best results are found in congregations where authoritative leadership is found in two or more of the cultural groups represented and a partnership formed with local leadership. Sometimes this is a pastor who has had to leave his/her own country, sometimes it is lay leadership. Many of the Christians from Nigeria who have come to Ireland come from a strong Pentecostal background which looks to charismatic leadership. The cooperation of these figures of authority is important.

*A Common Goal*

The common goal which requires great commitment on the part of both Irish and new residents is to experience real community with cultural diversity. It is important that the common goal of deepening fellowship is agreed and that suitable ways are found to achieve this. New immigrants are often separated from their family circles and therefore they want the Christian community that they join in Ireland to become for them a larger family where they can enjoy each other's company and find the security of belonging. They like to spend the greater part of Sunday together, worshipping, sharing a meal, talking and enjoying time together. Those who join some mainline Irish Churches are surprised at the short length of time spent together at worship. They find that Irish people are accustomed to one hour of worship at the most and then off to have a family dinner. Many immigrants find this a disappointing level of 'belonging together'. Matching these two traditions is a major challenge facing transcultural congregations. Some, finding the time spent together with fellow local members too short, also attend services of worship in migrant Churches from the same cultural and linguistic group.

One of the most important means of creating this sense of belonging to one family is to experience frequent sharing of meals. This is what a natural family does. It is necessary for the Christian family also. Narcisse expresses its importance:

> The first Christmas we were invited to a Christmas party by the local congregation. The next Christmas we invited them to an African Christmas party when we ate and sang together. These two meals were very important in sealing the commitment of the newcomers and traditional congregation to each other. We also had an excursion to Glendalough when we spent about 5 or 6 hours together and had a great time. It was very nice, very nice.

It is clear that expectations of in-depth interaction differ between African and Irish people assembling for worship. An African Christian in coming to attend a Church service may be looking forward to something akin to arriving at a relation's home to spend the day. They see a Christian congregation as an extended family with whom you want to spend time. The timing of the arrival is not very important. The activities of the day will include worship, singing together, sharing a meal, conversation and enjoyment of each other's company. An Irish Christian will attend worship as something that he/she wants to do or feels obliged to do for a fixed period of time. Even though done in the company of others, many Irish people still see worship more as a private act than as a social event.

The sense of being one family comes through sharing time and experiences together. It comes through caring for each other when any member is experiencing difficulties. For example, members of these congregations spend long hours helping others to fill in application forms and helping them through the difficult procedures required to gain recognition as refugees and, eventually, full citizenship.

Music is also a means of sharing. Many transcultural congregations have formed musical groups complete with drums and instruments from many parts of the world. They try to learn and sometimes mix different types of music for use in public worship. The experience of producing music together helps to promote a sense of belonging.

Pursuing common tasks together also increases a sense of belonging. In Killarney Methodist Church the new members have formed a rota to clean the church building instead of leaving that task to one or two of the original Irish members. In the congregation in Galway, joining together in running a Friendship Club for the benefit of other new immigrants who are not members of the congregation, is a common endeavour. A sense of belonging is greatly improved when each cultural group takes time to understand the other. Narcisse says, 'We need to learn English but we would like the Irish to learn something about us. It was gratifying to see an elderly Dubliner following the Scripture reading in a French Bible and finding after some time that she could understand to a degree what was being spoken in French. We add something to the Church and bring something new to the Irish Church.'

*Other Elements of Reconciliation; Forgiveness and Repentance*

When a number of different cultural groups come together to form one congregation there are inevitably misunderstandings and tensions. Sometimes hurt is caused unintentionally to one group by another due to a lack of understanding. If the group that is hurt does not forgive what has happened but allows resentment to increase this can cause serious division. Experience shows that in successful transcultural congregations misunderstandings, when they occur, are dealt with immediately and not swept under the carpet. Tony, a leader in a transcultural congregation in Dublin, speaks again:

> Where mistakes lead to misunderstandings we try to recognize the dominance of relationship. Where there is a good relationship and honesty and respect then we can begin to resolve these things. There are three stages: (1) Acknowledge that there has been a mistake that has caused hurt. This can be intuitive. (2) Analyse what has happened. This requires exploring exactly what has happened and why: the dynamics of the occurrence. (3) Find ways of resolving the issue. Sometimes it is very simple.

Narcisse from the Congo, a leader of one of the new cultural groups that has joined the same congregation, says: 'We need to talk to find out that they are only misunderstandings and not intentional acts. For example, in Africa you don't wait for an invitation to visit someone you know as a friend. It is normal just to call without invitation. In Ireland this is not so.'

Another common cause of friction is the tendency for African members to arrive late at services. Where it is not acknowledged and dealt with it can fester and cause a serious breakdown in relationships. In one congregation I visited in Waterford they solved the problem by appointing an African Grandpa to stand in the porch and only open the door at appropriate moments so as not to disturb the congregation.

Sometimes there are a lot of children at the service and one or two can get out of control. The noise level rises and this is another source of friction. Again, an African Granny was appointed to sit at the back and keep her eye on mothers who cannot keep all their children quiet at once. Granny slips into the pew and takes the child that is becoming noisy to another pew and has a picture book at hand.

When friction occurs it needs to be attended to and not ignored as if it hadn't happened. This is where good leadership is needed. Transcultural congregations work well when there is a leader of each cultural group and a close relationship of trust between them. This means that when relations get strained one leader can say to another, 'We acknowledge that that was the wrong thing to do. What can we do to put it right?'

In a Catholic parish in Limerick the following incident took place. Shortly after the arrival of a large group of asylum-seekers in the city a bus-tour was organized for them. Those who wanted to go were asked to write their names down on a list on a notice board. It was emphasized that only the first 14 would be able to go because of the size of the bus. The organizers were taken aback when on the day of the excursion 14 asylum-seekers turned up but none of them had written their name on the notice board. Those who had written their names on the board did not regard that act as an individual contract with the organizers. They saw it as something that required a collective decision by the whole group of asylum-seekers as to who should go.

This is an example of the western focus on the individual as opposed to the collective way of thinking prevalent in many other cultures. It is not dissimilar to the collective thinking of antiquity described above by Bruce Malina.[35] It certainly caused shock and some degree of hurt amongst those who had organized the event in Limerick. Even without fully understanding why this misunderstanding had arisen the organisers let the incident go in order to move on. When differences such as these are clarified, it is much easier to forgive and not allow resentment to build up.

35. See supra, p. 28.

Repenting, the changing of former attitudes and adopting new ones, can take time. Due to racism, as explained above, some lingering attitudes of paternalism remain for a time within most Irish people. Within a transcultural congregation these attitudes begin to disappear much more quickly than amongst a similar group of Irish people who do not have such close contact with other cultures. Tony maintains, 'There is now no outward sense of one group feeling superior to another in the congregation. However, when differences are not acknowledged or enough time given to understanding why there are differences, this implies that one group feels inwardly that their way of doing things is the only way.'

This assumption that our way is the only way of doing things is another form of paternalism that takes time to eradicate.

## RELATIONS BETWEEN LOCAL CHURCHES OF DIFFERENT CULTURES

Many new residents who have come to Ireland in recent years and who wish to have Christian fellowship join Christian Churches or fellowships with which they had connections in the country of their origin. It is only natural that many would seek the company of people from a similar linguistic/cultural and denominational background. A minority also join a transcultural congregation and maintain connections with both.

The number of Russian-speaking people now resident in the Dublin area is estimated as 15,000, many of whom have joined the Russian Orthodox Church which uses a former Church of Ireland parish building in Harold's Cross. The African migrant Churches have a membership estimated at between 30,000 and 40,000. According to a report produced for the Irish Council of Churches by Dr Femi Olayisade, they are mostly of Nigerian origin. The largest of these Churches is the Redeemed Christian Church of God, with 39 local churches and four regional pastors. The Mountain of Fire Ministries and Tower of Power Ministries, like the Redeemed Church of God, are Pentecostal. The Christ Apostolic Church is in the Apostolic tradition. There are also White Garment Churches with links to Churches in England of which The Church of the Cherubim and Seraphim is the most prominent. In addition there are many Christian Fellowships some times referred to as Africa Indigenous Churches.

*Proximity*

For such Churches and fellowship groups the first pressing problem is to find a place to meet. These independent Churches often look for a tenancy in traditional Churches that will give them freedom to organize their own affairs. Two or more congregations can worship in the same building but at different times. Sometimes an approach to a traditional Church meets with a negative response. This can be for a number of reasons; the congregation wants to encourage integration instead of a separate and perhaps competitive development or they are afraid of possible damage being done to their buildings. The result is that many migrant congregations have to look for accommodation in civic buildings or private houses.

Even where one or more migrant Churches share a Church building with a traditional Irish congregation relations have often not progressed as might have been hoped. The noise level that comes from many African styles of worship may cause friction. The expectation that African styles of worship will be the same as Irish styles of worship is not met. The tenant congregation does not feel responsible for cleaning up after using the premises and fails to realize that many Churches cannot afford cleaning staff and need to rely on voluntary help.

*Equality*

Local Churches usually charge a low rent for the use of buildings but any rental agreement sets up a landlord/tenant relationship. Churches Together in England have published guidelines on the sharing of buildings. Entitled *Sharers, Guests or Tenants,* it is available on their website: www.churches-together.org.uk). Relationships between traditional and migrant Churches, whether those using the same building or in the same neighbourhood, need sensitivity and patience.

At national level equality of treatment is also important. The Irish Council of Churches has recently welcomed the Coptic Orthodox, Greek Orthodox and Cherubim and Seraphim Churches into membership. Consultations are continuing with the Russian Orthodox and Romanian Orthodox Churches.

*Authority*

A Christian Leadership Network of migrant Church leaders has been established and one of its functions is to screen new leaders of Christian fellowships and congregations starting in the cities of Ireland. These Churches have different emphasises but all acknowledge Jesus Christ as Saviour and Lord. How to relate to some of these Churches that are very independent will pose problems not only for the mainstream Churches but also other migrant Churches. Femi Olayisade in his report to the Irish Council of Churches states:

> There is very little relationship between the White Garment Churches and the Pentecostals Churches and the Christ Apostolic Church. Between the two White Garment Churches there tends to be little relationship. Among Pentecostal Churches, there are relationships among the leaders but there are some elements of caution and suspicion and competition over members.

This all indicates that there is considerable diversity amongst the new Churches that have come to Ireland. There is one common authority in Jesus Christ but a wide variety of authoritative figures.

*Common Goals*

The Irish Council of Churches has arranged a number of meetings of the leaders of these migrant Churches. Issues concerning the status of asylum-seekers and other migrant workers have been discussed. This has resulted in a feeling amongst the leaders of migrant Churches that they can work with other Churches in the pursuit of some common goals. This association, though minimal, is vitally important if migrant congregations are not to become isolated and detached.

There is some evidence, especially in Germany, that some African and Asian migrant Churches are engaging in what is called 'reverse mission',[36] going into direct competition with the traditional Churches. Many European Churches are now, after a long period of neglect, beginning to focus attention on the importance of building good relations between the traditional Churches and the new migrant Churches within each state.

36. Claudia Wahrisch-Oblau, 'Together on the Way in Germany,' *Reformed World*, Vol. 50 No. 4 (Geneva, World Alliance of Reformed Churches, 2000) p. 187.

## 3. The Ephesian Moment

Andrew F. Walls defines the Ephesian Moment in the early Church as 'the social coming together of two cultures to experience Christ.'[37] It was made possible because people from two cultures lived in proximity in cosmopolitan cities of the Roman Empire. It was a moment that left a profound mark upon the church and Europe. It was a brief moment because circumstances changed. The Jewish state was destroyed leaving much recrimination between Jew and Gentile. After the moment was over the Church quite quickly became mono-cultural, overwhelmingly Hellenistic.

Another example of an Ephesian Moment was the period in North America when people from African cultures who were slaves to landowners/ farmers worshipped for a time together with their masters in one building though segregated. Professor Willie Ruff of Yale University propounds the interesting theory that Gospel music had its origins in this period when African Christians worshipped in Presbyterian churches where Gaelic was spoken. The Presbyterian Gaelic speakers sang with a precentor leading in a style of music known as *line out.* When eventually Black Churches separated from white they continued with this style of music adapted to suit their culture and situation. Thus he maintains the Gospel music of today owes its origins to two cultures meeting even in a restricted segregated way. Dr Michael Newton who teaches at Richmond and Virginia Commonwealth University, USA, maintains that 'few people are even dimly aware of the complex ways in which early Americans of all sorts enriched each other's traditions.'[38]

Today we have a new Ephesian Moment in the cosmopolitan cities of Europe, USA and many other places. This time it is not just two cultures that are meeting but many. This time the Christian community has spread to Africa, Asia and Latin America so that many of those who have come to the cities of the West from these areas are Christians. In addition to the Christians who have come to settle in Ireland from various countries in Africa, Asia and Eastern Europe there are at least 20,000 Muslims from

37. Andrew F. Walls, *The Cross-cultural Process in Christian History* (Mary Knoll, New York: Orbis Books; and Edinburgh: T&T Clark, 2002) p. 78.

38. *History of Scotland,* March/April, 2005.

Middle Eastern countries and the Sudan. In Amsterdam by 2010 it is expected that half of the under-thirties in a population of 1 million will be non-Dutch.

The risks people take to reach Europe indicate that many have reached desperation point in their home countries. Some 3,000 people have died trying to gain entry to Europe. Many die at sea in overcrowded boats and some have literally fallen out of airplane undercarriages. Removing all control over the numbers of immigrants coming to Europe is probably not a solution but if this is accepted then a far greater urgency is needed in tackling the causes of emigration from developing countries. Making international trade regulations fairer must be a top priority so that wealth and employment can be created in developing countries.

The number of asylum seekers in Ireland is decreasing. The government now appears to be embarking on a policy that the Irish Bishops' Committee on Asylum Seekers and Refugees calls 'Pre-emptive Exclusion.' The central principle that determines Irish asylum procedure is the applicant's need for protection. This however only comes into force after an application has been lodged. This application can only be made within the state or at its frontiers, not outside. The Government is also making it an offence for carriers to bring 'improperly documented' passengers into the state on the grounds that they should apply for asylum elsewhere in the EU. Thus the effect of this policy is to erect a 'glass wall of exclusion around Ireland.'[39] It is not, therefore, surprising that the number of asylum-seekers coming to Ireland as opposed to migrant workers, has dropped considerably in recent years. Questions have to be raised as to the fairness of the treatment of potential refugees.

Yet the population in Europe and most other developed countries is projected to fall: in Germany by 14%, in Italy by 25%, in Russia and the Ukraine by as much as 40%.[40] Migration will be needed to maintain standards of living. In Ireland the population is not expected to fall so dramatically but if the economy continues to grow migrant workers will be needed. The number of people coming into the country with work permits and as a right through membership of the EU, is increasing. For

39. Statements on Asylum and Refugee Issues by the Irish Bishop's Committee, 1999-2001, *Refugees and Asylum Seekers – a Challenge to Solidarity*, (The Irish Commission for Justice and Peace/Trocaire, 2002) p. 82.

40. United Nations Report on Population, 2001.

these reasons, the cities of Ireland are likely to remain cosmopolitan.

The opportunities for further integration and mutual enrichment are there and are likely to remain. Will they be taken? How should we proceed? The following comments are focused mainly on the Republic of Ireland but may well be applicable in other countries.

## GRASPING THE EPHESIAN MOMENT IN THE STATE

The arrival of asylum-seekers and migrant workers into many parts of Europe has brought a rich diversity of people to many countries but it has also in some places brought tension, xenophobia and sometimes a violent reaction. The EU has produced a useful Handbook[41] to help those seeking to bring about integration. There is general recognition that much more needs to be done.

The Department of Justice, Equality and Law Reform launched *Planning for Diversity: the National Action Plan against Racism* (NAPR)[42] in February 2005. The plan is comprehensive and seeks to develop a more inclusive, intercultural society in Ireland. It seeks to provide a commendable intercultural framework of Protection, Inclusion, Provision, Participation and Recognition. By highlighting the Allport elements I hope to show how it may be possible to take some steps beyond combating racism and towards a deeper integration.

Much of what follows has been said by various organizations concerned about the treatment of asylum seekers, refugees and migrant workers and by many individuals, but by using the Allport elements for integration as headings I hope to show what are the essentials of any strategy for integration and indicate some of the current government policies which may mitigate against the NAPR.

### *Acquaintance potential*

Social harmony can only be developed when people are given the opportunity to meet regularly. On the whole, it is the initiative of schools, sports clubs, local Churches, art centres and individuals that makes this possible. Schools and colleges bring people together of all ages and from different cultural, religious and ethnic backgrounds. Some primary and

41. *Handbook on Integration,* Directorate-General Justice, Freedom and Security, 2004
42. *Planning for Diversity,* Department of Justice, Equality and Law Reform, 2005.

secondary schools have become transcultural and are making a considerable contribution towards integration. The example of Palmerston Community School teachers and students successfully campaigning again the deportation of a Nigerian student indicates the degree of integration achieved in that school. At third level, there are opportunities in societies and sports clubs for integration where students so desire. Not all take these opportunities. A minority of Muslim students keep as separate as possible, even desiring to play football only amongst themselves. In England integration in schools and colleges is the state policy but in some areas, such as Bradford, in practice schools come to be predominantly of one culture or another.

The work place can also be where integration occurs. This, of course, varies according to the policy of the management, problems with language, and degree of prejudice. Many of the new industries that have come to Ireland, pursue a policy that gives equal opportunity to all and results in international workforces. As far back as 1953, T.J.Watson Jr, one of the founders of IBM, wrote in a policy letter: 'It is the policy of this organization to hire people who have the personality, talent and background necessary to fill a given job, regardless of race, colour or creed.'[43] This policy is common among the new industries and has now spread to native Irish industries especially the service and construction industries and certain types of farming.

The current government policy of not allowing asylum-seekers to work deprives them of the experience of mixing with Irish and other workers for months and years while waiting for 'leave to stay' or the status of 'refugee', and is a factor in hindering their integration. The process of acquiring the status of refugee is very slow.

Peter O'Mahony, Chief Executive Officer of the Irish Refugee Council, wrote,

> Without a real commitment to the integration of those who have sought refuge in Ireland, many of whom will be long-term residents of Ireland, there is a real risk that a new underclass will develop that is resented by others in the community and that is resentful of its exclusion from mainstream society. Over time this runs the real risk of fes-

43. *IBM Annual Report* 2001 (IBM, 2001)

tering and the shortsighted current policies that ultimately lead to social exclusion will have a long-term cost. The lack of routine contact between Irish people and asylum seekers and the superficiality of much of the media coverage allows the perception to develop that large numbers of asylum-seekers are spongers and serious wrongdoers; the reality is that, while some may be, most are not. Nothing militates against the integration of refugees and asylum-seekers in Ireland as much as the Government's policy that prevents all asylum-seekers taking up paid employment. This is despite the fact that groups such as the Congress of Trades Unions, IBEC and the National Organisation of the Unemployed have signed up to a call that asylum-seekers should be allowed to work if their applications remain unprocessed after a six-month period.[44]

State grants are available for cultural events to bring people together but more grants are needed to provide, for example, transport, for asylum-seekers and migrant workers living separately from the rest of the population to social events where they can mix regularly with Irish people. Making it easier for people to meet on a regular basis is one essential element on the road to integration.

*Equality*

Unequal treatment of migrant workers is a serious hindrance to building up good relationships. Integration requires that migrants are treated fairly and not exploited. Examples have come to light of wages being paid to migrant workers that are well below the minimum wage, and of landlords refusing accommodation when they see the colour of a person's skin. It must be said that the media have exposed some of these examples and steps have been taken to rectify inequalities in wages and treatment of foreign workers.

The July 2003 issue of *Sanctuary* points out:

> The UN Convention on the Rights of All Migrant Workers and their Families came into force on 1 July 2003 – regrettably, no EU member is among the 20 states that ratified the Convention, thus making it

44. *World Refugee Day – A Chance to Reflect on a Little Done but a Lot to Do,* Irish Times, 20 June 2003.

enforceable. More than 150 million migrants (2% of the world's population) – migrant workers, refugees, asylum seekers, permanent immigrants and others – live and work in a country other than that of their birth or citizenship.[45]

However, there are many places of work with very diverse workforces where integration is slowly taking place in so far as language and time permit. When management treats migrant workers fairly and, by example, creates an atmosphere of acceptance most Irish workers respond and collegiality grows. Since the ability to speak English is linked to the speed of integration in the work place more language classes are needed on industrial estates.

Patrick Taran and August Gachter [46] have produced an 'agenda for action' with regard to equality of treatment in the workplace. They name a number of objectives to promote workplace equality:

Migrant workers should be supported in adapting to the workplace.

Cultural diversity should be acknowledged with initiatives taken to accommodate the practical implications.

The majority workforce should be supported to explore, and change if necessary, their attitudes to migrant workers and to cultural diversity.

The majority workforce should be appropriately supported, and required as necessary, not to discriminate against or harass black and minority ethnic workers.

Workplace rules and procedures should be developed as necessary to promote equality in practice.

The state should encourage the furtherance of these objectives with grants where necessary and by financing an adequate inspection of places of work to ensure that malpractice does not take place.

*Authority*

The authority of the state is exercised in two main areas. It controls who enters the state and it shows hospitality to those who come seeking refugee status, to refugees and some migrant workers.

45. *Sanctuary*, issued by the Refugee Project of the Irish Bishops' Conference, 2003.
46. *Achieving Equality in Intercultural Workplaces*, Equality Authority in Ireland 2003.

Immigration control policy attracts more notice than does hospitality. Many states give the impression that keeping the immigrant levels as low as possible is their top priority. Ireland, while receiving many migrant workers, keeps the levels of asylum-seekers very low: figures for the third quarter of 2004 indicate that Ireland received less than half the number of asylum-seekers of either Cyprus or Slovakia in that period. The same figures put Ireland into sixteenth place, behind Poland, in the league of new applications for asylum in the industrialised world. While claiming not to be racist, policy seems to be directed to keeping the numbers from non-EU countries as low as possible.

When asylum-seekers do arrive they are not allowed to work while waiting to be given the status of 'refugee' and while waiting for 'leave to stay'. This may take years to achieve. The ban on working is justified on the grounds that it will discourage other asylum-seekers from coming to Ireland. There is little evidence that the level of welfare is a priority when people are choosing a country in which to seek asylum. According to a UNHCR statement of 2000, 'asylum-seekers, when deciding where to lodge their application, are more swayed by the presence of their own community than by the reception standards and benefits.'

Taken together with deportation orders, sometimes served on those who have had a long stay in the country, the impression is given that the authority of the state is directed towards allowing into the country as many temporary workers as are needed but discouraging asylum-seekers from finding a new home in Ireland.

When thinking about hospitality policy, it is important to note that Ireland, having signed up to the 1951 Geneva Convention on Refugees, has an obligation to show hospitality to the asylum seeker and refugee. The state carries out this obligation by providing accommodation and a small weekly grant. The special accommodation sometimes has the effect of isolating asylum-seekers. The accommodation is not meant to be a prison; but local managers through various restrictions can make it feel like imprisonment to those who live there. The smallness of the weekly grant also means asylum-seekers have little money left for socializing. Perhaps the most serious effect is to demoralize and depress those so treated. Since a majority of the general public do not make distinctions between asylum-seekers and other 'foreigners', the authority of the state is thus not perceived as firmly behind a policy of hospitality leading to greater integration.

Integration cannot be forced on a population but government can give general authority to the process. If a daily diet of asylum-seeker scare stories and deportations is to be combated, governments need to proclaim publicly their obligation on behalf of the state to give hospitality to asylum-seekers. As a signatory to the 1951 Geneva Convention on Refugees, the state needs constantly to remind citizens of this obligation in order to impress upon people that this obligation has the authority of the Irish government and of the international community.

There is a tension between this general obligation to give hospitality and the practical regulatory system that a state needs to control numbers. It is our contention that both need to be given authorisation by the state

French philosopher Jacques Derrida has written about this dilemma.[47] The context of Derrida's discussion is the cosmopolitan city that is open to newcomers yet in the present day must have some restrictions. How can the tensions between refugee and asylum rights and the ethic of hospitality be resolved?

Jacques Derrida refers to the biblical vision in the Book of Numbers where God says to Moses: 'Speak to the Israelites and say, ...these six towns will serve as refuge for the Israelites, for the foreigner and for the resident alien, where anyone who has accidentally killed someone can take sanctuary' (Num 35:15). He then states that Pauline Christianity radicalised this Hebrew concept within the Christian Church: Gentiles are 'no longer foreigners nor strangers in a foreign land, but fellow citizen with God's people, members of God's household' (Eph 2:19).

This Christian obligation to hospitality has been secularised to the extent that Kant regarded the obligation to give hospitality to anyone 'from the surface of the earth' as a natural law. [48] Kant then produced two conditions: He excluded hospitality as meaning a right of residence.; it was only a right of visitation. He made the right of residence depend-

47. Jacques Derrida, *Cosmopolitanism and Forgiveness* (London and New York: Routledge, 2001), p. 8.

48. Immanuel Kant, *Perpetual Peace: A Philosophical Essay*, trans. M. Campbell Smith (New York and London: Garland Publishing Inc., 1972), pp. 137-8.

ent on state law. The term 'natural law' is open to question; but today the international community as a rule tries to take the principle of hospitality seriously.

A problem facing any government is that, apart from the practical need to have some restriction on numbers entering the jurisdiction, citizens of a state can become fearful of being swamped or deprived of work or benefits from too generous a hospitality. In a democratic state this leads the government to aspire, at least publicly, to a strict policy on asylum-seekers rather than appear weak. Derrida suggests that it is a matter of transforming and improving state laws while at the same time accepting the principle of unconditional hospitality offered to every *other.* He admits that this position is uncomfortable if not contradictory, but can see no way of avoiding it.

Popular opinion in countries that have experienced racial disturbance in recent years is that the numbers of immigrants allowed into the country is to blame. In fact, the real cause may be lack of effort to integrate. These issues are being discussed in many European countries; but there is, as yet, no common EU immigration policy. It is to be hoped that whatever policy is reached a balance is found between the need to control immigration and the obligation to show hospitality leading to integration and thus eradicating many fears.

Perhaps most important of all is that the state should be open about what it is doing, and, along with every change in legislation limiting numbers, also state the equally important principle of hospitality. Otherwise, the authority of the state is removed from the principle of hospitality, and people hear only about the latest restrictions or deportations. The result is that not only do people resent asylum-seekers, they lump all 'foreign' workers with asylum seekers making integration for all more difficult.

*Common Goals*

Integration works best where there are common goals. Some of the best projects for integrating young people from various backgrounds are team sports where all obviously have a common goal. Such projects deserve state support. Well-managed businesses seek to create amongst all staff a sense of working for a common goal. The state too needs to create a feeling amongst all who reside within its bounds that they are working for a common good and their efforts are appreciated. Perhaps awards for those who have taken successful initiatives in integration, open to people of whatever status or ethnic group, would help to convey a sense of everyone working for a common goal.

*Forgiveness, Repentance and Reconciliation*

The four Allport elements are necessary to bring about a degree of integration in society. However, there are other elements that in some circumstances are also important. Jacques Derrida points out that the terms 'forgiveness, repentance, confession and apology' have broken out of their religious boxes; and what is happening, he says, 'resembles an immense scene of confession in progress, thus a virtually Christian convulsion-conversion-confession, a process of Christianisation which has no more need for the Christian Church.'[49] While not agreeing that the Christian Church has become obsolete, one welcomes the fact that these terms have come into more general usage.

A cosmopolitan city will have many ethnic groups some of whom may have had periods of conflict in the past. The racism that exists in Ireland has been handed down from times when one race felt superior to another. Integration, therefore, requires some degree of forgiveness. If there is to be integration or harmonious living alongside each other, there is need for a 'letting go' of past enmity and also a repenting of feelings of superiority. There needs to be a desire to move on to building new relations, a new city.

Miroslav Volf uses the term 'embrace'[50] to signify this unconditional forgiveness and acceptance. New residents need to be embraced, welcomed, and made to feel at home. Good political leadership can go some way towards conveying this. More open gestures of 'embrace', of unconditional acceptance of people who have come from overseas to live in Ireland would help to create an atmosphere in which integration can be pursued. Many African cultures lay emphasis on 'welcoming' ceremonies. There is a real tension between those who want to embrace the newcomer unconditionally and those who first want to see if they will become like us. If their behaviour is obviously different and non-con-

49. Derrida, p. 31.

50. Miroslav Volf, *Exclusion and Embrace* (Maryknoll, New York: Orbis Books; Edinburgh: T&T Clark, 2002), p. 164

forming the embrace is withheld. Yet integration should not mean that those who are different must become like us (total assimilation).

Some politicians in Ireland have offered apologies after racist attacks have occurred. It is needed because four out of five people from ethnic minorities have been the victims of racism while living in Ireland.[51] A Minister for Justice apologized to the Jewish community for the refusal of Ireland to receive Jewish refugees before and after the Holocaust. This helps to repair relationships.

Many states, including Ireland, would now describe themselves as transcultural. The term *transcultural* has sometimes meant nothing more than a variety of different cultures living in one place. Without initiatives to form new relationships between the various groups, a transcultural society can become a series of small social circles without much interaction between them. Each of the elements required to encourage integration requires support from the government to encourage and facilitate greater achievement.

## GRASPING THE EPHESIAN MOMENT IN THE CHURCH

Can the Churches give hope that differences must not always lead to conflict?

If society finds it difficult to put these elements of integration into practice then this increases the responsibility of the Churches to put them into practice under the authority of Jesus Christ. If society is afraid that too much integration might mean some changes, this increases the responsibility on local Churches to experience trans-cultural togetherness to such an extent that change is accepted. If society is afraid that too much cultural diversity would threaten unity then this increases the responsibility of local Churches to discover unity in Christ with diversity.

Jacques Derrida writes about the ethic of hospitality. An ethic needs to be subscribed to in order to be effective. If people live in an environment where the dangers of hospitality are constantly brought before them the ethic of hospitality will fade unless the state acknowledges this ethic and the United Nations Declaration on Refugees is brought to public attention. This means that the Churches which have deep within their tradition the importance of giving hospitality to the stranger (Deut 10:19)

51. *Amnesty Survey* 2001

have a special responsibility to the stranger in our midst and to the formation of a community which accepts diversity without fear. For the Christian community the ethic of hospitality arises out of first experiencing God's hospitality. As Miroslav Volf puts it, 'God's reception of hostile humanity into divine communion is a model for how human beings should relate to the other.'[52]

Only if congregations and Churches at local and national level move beyond a mono-cultural existence and discover a unity not based on ethnicity or uniformity, but on a common relationship to Jesus Christ, will they in turn attract attention and be taken seriously by the rest of society. With the experience and integrity of their own practice the Churches will then be able to act as advocates on behalf of the refugee and the stranger in partnership with other organizations and groups who feel the same.

Will today's new Ephesian Moment within the Christian community be able to give hope to the world that conflict is not irreversible? People in situations of long-drawn-out conflict are frequently condemned to despair. They feel that there is no escape, that it is just the nature of things. Others who see the homogeneous society of a former age beginning to pass away feel threatened and depressed. Christian hope can keep people from despair and cynicism. It can sustain people to keep seeking for a city, not one that we design but one whose architect and builder is God. Hope is necessary if we are to continue to strive for partial anticipations of the city of peace. Even partial anticipations give people a taste of what is to come.

## GRASPING THE EPHESIAN MOMENT IN LOCAL TRANS-CULTURAL CHURCHES

### *Proximity*

Trans-cultural congregations are significant for the Church and for society. They will come about where newcomers feel welcome. The initial welcome can be crucial. Many trans-cultural local Churches refer to a *kairos* moment – a meal, a social event, a special celebration – when two or more culturally different groups begin to bond together, finding their unity in Christ.

52. Miroslav Volf, *op. cit.*, p. 100.

While the initial welcome is important, what happens next is equally important. In a house when people are invited as guests they usually have to try and accommodate the hosts' wishes and adapt to the pattern and customs of the house. But if those who come are not guests but have become members who belong to the house, some things will change. There will need to be some redecorating and renovating, perhaps some additional rooms added. Being a trans-cultural local Church means seeing how 'our' house needs to change.

Helen Richmond writes from an experience of transcultural ministry in Sydney, Australia:

> 'Hospitality' is a helpful concept but it needs to be used carefully as it sometimes carries with it the notion of 'host and guest.' If by 'hospitality' we mean *us* welcoming others into *our* house then this is a metaphor of limited value. But if we understand the house to belong to God, then together with God we work to build a house where *all* belong, open to giving and receiving from each other. It means everyone must be open to change and ready to adapt, not just expect others to fit into our way of doing things. As we share meals together we begin to see the stranger not as a threat nor as someone who diminishes our life but as someone who becomes a channel of God's grace. A multi-cultural congregation is on a journey together learning to be a community that shows the hospitality of Christ and shares fairly the resources.[53]

Fr Philip Sumner, now working in St Patrick's Roman Catholic Church in Oldham and with many years of experience in Moss Side, Manchester, makes these recommendations:

1. Liturgy and Church art should reflect the universality of the Church and celebrate diversity in communion.
2. Racial and ethnic identities need to be valued and nurtured within Church institutions, but in an inclusive way.
3. Those who exercise ministries within the Church should reflect the ethnic make-up of the worshipping community.[54]

53. Helen Richmond, 'Struggles in Multi-Cultural Ministry,' *Multicultural Ministry* (Sydney: Inform, 2002), p. 18.

54. *Out-Caste to Authority*, (London: Catholic Association for Racial Justice, 2002), p. 25.

In Ireland various styles of music that represent the variety of cultures present have invigorated the worship of many trans-cultural local Churches and shown that members of these different cultural groups are equally valued.

Since it is likely that in many large cities throughout the world the populations will continue to be of mixed origins this will provide opportunities for both traditional and migrant Churches and Christian fellowships to welcome into their membership people from numerous backgrounds. Within these trans-cultural local Churches they can begin to learn from each other and be thereby enriched. In this way Christians now have the opportunity to break out of the inhibiting mono-cultural membership that many have come to regard as normal

In Amsterdam it is reported that 'older empty' churches are again filled with new often black believers and that the few remaining white believers enjoy the way in which their church can experience such a kind of 'rebirth' and 'resurrection'. On a small scale in these churches a certain sense of integration is growing. [55]

It is also reported from Holland that within some Moluccan Churches, despite for many years receiving little attention from the established Churches, 'there are now active "indigenous" members of the congregation and church councils.' [56] Indeed it may be true that many of the young immigrant Churches are more open to integrate strangers than the traditional Churches.

*Equality of Treatment*

For those local Churches that embark on this experiment it will mean that new members from other cultures must soon be given equal status to older members. In other words, membership will involve some kind of re-socialization. It will be very challenging in that everyone concerned will have to share the pain of those who are different and of those who are disturbed by change. Unless both traditional members and new members cry each others' tears they can never be one together.

55. M. E Brinkman, 'Is There Any Faith in the City?' *Culture Divides – the Gospel Unites?* (Brussels: Churches' Commission for Migrants in Europe, 2002), p. 27.

56. Brinkman, *art. cit*, p. 76.

*International Equality*

The missionary movement of the last few centuries has brought about a situation where we now have not just two cultures, as in the early Church, but innumerable cultures within the world Church. New Christian life-styles and expressions of Christianity have developed in Africa, Asia and Latin America under the Spirit; and Christians in the West must seek to relate to them. The majority of Christians now live outside the western world. Western Christians can no longer regard their expression of Christianity as 'standard' nor are we are free to isolate ourselves. As V.S Azariah, a Christian leader from South India, said to Western Church leaders in Edinburgh in 1910, 'Give us friends.' [57] Friendship requires equality and mutual respect. Many Christians in the West have not yet assimilated the international nature of the Church. Patronizing attitudes must end and friendships must be built up with other Christians from many cultures, recognizing that their expressions of Christianity are as valid as Western expressions.

In many countries language is a barrier to the formation of trans-cultural local Churches. In Ireland a minority of trans-cultural local Churches use more than one language. Some use interpreters after sermons or prayers and others use simultaneous translation. The use of more than one language is a sign of equality. Where it is needed, the use of more than one language should become a normal part of our Church meetings.

*Authority*

As Church members encounter differences within their Christian communities they need to find their unity in Christ. They need to be able to distinguish between what is essential to the faith and cultural expressions of it. All Church members need to listen for the Word of God, expecting challenge and a call for change. Preachers and Bible Study leaders need to help members to understand the changes that are taking place as part of God's plan. The Ephesian Moment needs to be understood not as the end of everything but the beginning of something new that has authorization from the Scriptures, tradition and the Spirit.

To help members cope with the changes in their Christian commu-

57. Andrew F. Walls, *op. cit*, p. 70.

nity they need authoritative teaching. Theological reflection is needed on this new Ephesian Moment. It will surely be found that a theology of receiving needs to be developed. This will emphasize such themes as hospitality and a consciousness of the importance of the stranger. Greater diversity in styles of worship so as to receive expressions, symbols and gestures from people of different cultures will also result in the need for reflection on what are the essential elements of worship.

When the Christian faith crossed the cultural boundary that separated Jew from Gentile new categories had to be found to express in theological terms what Christians were experiencing. Significantly they used metaphors from both cultures. They continued to use the Hebrew title, 'Messiah' but also 'Lord' (*Kyrios*), a Greek word. Similarly, when Christians today experience more fully the trans-cultural nature of the Church new categories will have to be found. Creative theology will become necessary. The Ephesian Christians found that Christ's stature was increased, not threatened, as they contemplated how Christ was able to bring such diversity into a new unity. Perhaps that will result again from greater contact between people from different cultural backgrounds. Some categories may come into greater use from a rediscovery of metaphors such as 'body' and 'household', used during the first Ephesian Moment. It is likely that new categories from Africa and Asia may be used in new theologies. Andrew F. Walls writes:

> The materials for constructing theology will be African and Asian, as surely as earlier generations used the material of Platonism and Roman customary law. If past experience is anything to go by, the process can only enrich the Church's understanding of Christ.[58]

An example of an African word that could profitably be used in Christian theological reflection is *Ubuntu,* which means 'generous', 'hospitable', 'caring' and 'compassionate'. It also means 'my humanity is caught up, bound up, in yours'. We belong in a bundle of life. A person is a person through other people. It is not 'I think therefore I am' but 'I am human because I belong.' Such a concept could be used to counter the emphasis on the individual in Western Christianity.

The Churches, by providing a place where there is not only accept-

58. Andrew F. Walls, *op. cit,* p. 81.

ance of difference but also a real encounter and struggle to live as one household for all the saints (Eph 3:17-19), can act as a model for living together. However to do this, local Churches experiencing a trans-cultural community today need to find authority for what they are doing in the teaching and actions of Jesus, in the experiences of the early Church in Ephesus and other cosmopolitan cities, and in other trans-cultural Churches throughout the world. They need to experience the guidance of the Spirit. They also need to reflect on what they are experiencing so that they understand what is happening and why.

*Common Goal*

Members of a trans-cultural Church need to have a common vision or goal of a community in which there are no longer strangers. This does not mean forced conformity to one theology, culture or style of worship. It does mean taking seriously any misunderstandings or disputes that might fracture the new household where there are no strangers. Whether it is disagreements based on differences of doctrine, class, culture or just personalities clashing, emphasis should be laid on resolving disputes within the Church. Trans-cultural local Churches by their very nature will bring clashes of culture, misunderstandings and stress. They must practise reconciliation if they are to continue. In the Western tradition of Christianity much emphasis has been put on each individual receiving God's forgiveness but it is also important to practice forgiveness and the resolution of disputes for the sake of the new community as a whole.

Conflict, being part of life, is part of being Church; so we need to learn how to handle it. The goal will be to heal what is strained and perhaps torn. The method is described very succinctly in Matthew 18. Where there is a dispute there are four steps that can be taken: (1) go directly to the person with whom you are in dispute; (2) if that step does not work take some witnesses; (3) if this fails bring the dispute out into the open before the whole congregation; (4) if all this fails relate to the person with whom you are in dispute as to a Gentile or tax-collector. At first this may sound like advice to ostracize them; but consider what Jesus did in relating to Gentiles and tax-collectors; he ate with them.[59]

The common goal of working to build up a new trans-cultural com-

59. John Paul Lederach, *The Journey toward Reconciliation* (Scottdale, Pennsylvania; Waterloo, Ontario, Herald Press, 1999), p. 118.

munity requires a commitment to the practice of reconciliation on the part of everyone. This applies to the long-term members and to those who have come recently. The minister of such a Church paid the following tribute about a member who arrived recently from Nigeria:

> One of the priorities of the Church was to have an integrated community of cultures from many ethnic backgrounds and Florence has certainly helped us achieve this. Through her shop, her visits, and her engaging personality she has invited people into the life of the Church. She has then nurtured them as they have developed their relationship with Christ, and His Church. She has been a 'bridge person' between the Irish and African cultures, along with a number of other African, and non-African, members of our congregation.[60]

## GRASPING THE EPHESIAN MOMENT TO BUILD GOOD RELATIONS BETWEEN CULTURALLY DIFFERENT SEPARATE CHRISTIAN COMMUNITIES AND PEOPLE OF DIFFERENT FAITHS

### *Proximity*

Sharing a common building by two or more culturally different congregations can be difficult. On the other hand, the potential for building up good relations is there if it can be grasped. Claudia Wahrisch-Oblau describes a cooperative venture in Essen in Germany where four Christian communities share one building:

> The blue and white square building sitting between the highway and the railway tracks does not look like a church at all. But the Weigle-Haus in Essen, named after its founding pastor, is a church, albeit a rather unusual one. Founded as an inner city youth ministry more than 100 years ago, it has long since developed into a congregation of sorts, or, in the words of its current pastor: 'into one church with four local churches.' First, there is the 'normal' Sunday morning congregation, consisting mostly of young adults and older people. Then there is the youth congregation that meets on Sunday nights. A few years ago, an African congregation asked for rooms at the Weigle-Haus. It was not just given a place; it has become part of the whole set-up. And when the German pastor learned that a Tamil congregation was com-

60. Correspondence from David Range, used with permission.

ing into existence, he specifically invited it to meet at the Weigle-Haus, too.

There was a reason for this: the Weigle-Haus has long been active in both social and evangelistic outreach to young people in Essen's inner city. Many of the youth living in the vicinity of the church are the children of Tamil refugees who have sought asylum in Germany. To help them cope with their schoolwork and improve their language abilities, the Weigle-Haus set up an after-school programme. Children and youth can do their homework at the church under supervision and get help if needed. But the church also wanted to reach out to the parents - and failed, as most Tamil refugees speak little or no German. Now the Tamil congregation has taken over the outreach to the Tamil parents: no more language problems!

The cooperation of the four local churches at the Weigle-Haus is quite unusual. After all, the German local churches are mainline evangelical (if with a strong evangelistic impulse), while both the African and the Tamil churches are neo-Pentecostal. The differences in theology and style are acknowledged and talked about on all levels. This way, understanding slowly grows while each church keeps its characteristics.

Occasionally, all four churches have a joint worship service. All the churches love them and would like to have them on a regular basis, but the pastors and church workers are not quite ready for this yet: 'Such services just take too much time to plan and prepare', sighs one German church worker who nevertheless admits that she loves the intercultural contact with the Africans and the Tamils.

This summer, a black church worker from the African congregation, who is currently undergoing theological training at a seminary in Belgium, did a month-long internship at the Weigle-Haus. Together with the church's full-time street worker, he established contacts with immigrant children and youth hanging out on street corners and game parlours. When he suggested running a drumming workshop, the response was enthusiastic. Street kids who had never responded to the German street worker came in droves and just loved every minute of the sessions. Now, the Weigle-Haus is thinking of establishing a longer term 'united in mission team' of immigrant and German street workers for this kind of outreach.[61]

This encouraging example has grasped the element of proximity and is working on matters to do with equality, authority and common mission.

Grasping the opportunities that arise from sharing a building has gone a step further in Bradford, England. Bradford has a population of 500,000 of whom 100,000 are Muslim. Unemployment is high at about 25%. There have been communal riots in recent years. Drugs are widely used and illegally sold. The resultant lawlessness means that there is a general sense of hopelessness in the area.

An old Anglican church in an interface area was classified as a dangerous building. Instead of abandoning the area or simply putting up a similar building, consultations were held and the bishop appointed Revd Paul Hackwood to oversee an imaginative project that would benefit the whole area. They asked an architect to design a centre in a way that made it open to the whole community but also gave the local Anglican community some private space to use as a congregation. The resulting building, the Thornbury Centre, was opened in April 1999. With large numbers of Muslims, Silks, Hindus and Christians, this area presents problems of inter-faith relationships that are challenging in a different way from those treated above. Yet within limits an initiative has been taken to bring reconciliation between people divided along religious lines.

The architect created an extremely light and airy building with a central atrium, which links all the rooms in the building. Everyone using the building needs to walk through the central communal area. What that does is create connections and it means that the ethos of the building is the same as that of the overall work – to create connections between people.

As you enter the building you step into a cafeteria area, a space that is meant to welcome people, and food is very welcoming. On the left is the worship area, which is entered through a stained glass door so as to give the impression of something special. At the back of the building is a community hall and bar, used for local celebrations. In addition there are seven meeting-rooms of varying sizes. Some of these are used by the projects that work from the building, and others are let out to other

61. Claudia Wahrisch-Oblau, 'Together on the Way in Germany', *Reformed World*, Vol. 50, No. 4 (December 2000), p. 188.

local organisations and businesses.

Those who run the Centre believe it is morally wrong to make the use of any service provided in the Centre dependent upon a faith allegiance. Everyone who comes to the centre is treated equally and, as far as possible, fairly.

The Anglican Church has an area over which it has full control, and has set up a charity that is made up of seven representatives from the church council, two from the local authority, three from the local community (including people of other faiths), four who represent the users of the centre, and one from the local school. The Church has a major say in what goes on though legally they have only a minority of the votes. With so many community representatives having a say in what goes on in the centre, the decisions taken by the charity have a lot of authority

The representatives of the various faith communities in Bradford who run the centre are all concerned to tackle the underlying problems that threaten the whole community. One of these is a very high unemployment rate. They run a café to provide a meeting place for all who use the building but they also train people in catering skills. Many people from the area have benefited and gone on to find permanent work. Those involved in running the centre all see the need for better understanding and relationships in the area. The numbers attending inter-faith meetings, seminars and conferences are high.

Relationships across the ethnic communities in Bradford are so bad they have a dehumanising influence on the whole of the neighbourhood. People are so alienated that, for example, Muslims won't have any contact with Hindus and Sikhs, whilst many young white English people won't even walk down streets where the Muslims live, and *vice versa.* The staff of Thornbury Centre tries to address these issues by working hard with the other religious communities. They have seen great progress led by a South Indian pastor who has a lot of knowledge of other faiths. Meetings and conferences have been organized on terrorism, jihad, and other critical issues. That progress is being made even in the aftermath of the Iraq war is demonstrated by what a group of Muslim leaders said, 'The Church of England is good news for this community.' [62]

62. Steve Chalke, 'Thornbury Centre,' in *Stories around the W orld* edited by Keith Danby,(UK, Authentic Media, 2002), p. 205.

No attempt has been made in the Thornbury Centre to formally engage in acts of forgiveness or repentance amongst representatives of the different faiths. They do not organize or participate in inter-faith worship. Yet relations amongst those who use the building are gradually improving.

The Thornbury Centre is producing a little flicker of hope in an area that has very little. Paul Hackwood writes:

> What we are really trying to do is to create an alternative. I don't think we can ever change the whole world, or even, for that matter, the whole of Thornbury. But we can create an alternative that says there is a different way to live and relate to others; you don't have to live solely for your own survival; it's possible to live in a way where you trust others and are prepared to listen and work together with them.[63]

In this project, as in Weigle-Haus, good leadership has taken the initiative and using the first element of reconciliation, proximity, is working on other elements as far as possible.

These two examples should not give the impression that simply sharing a building will bring closer relationships. It is, unfortunately, a fact that sharing a building has been the cause of much friction in Ireland and many parts of the world. To ensure that premises left untidy after meetings and other events do not result in a breakdown in relations it is necessary that leaders meet regularly to deal with the causes of friction. (See *Sharers, Guests or Tenants,* on www.churches-together.org.uk)

*Equality*

There is need within the mainline Churches for 'recognition' at local level of pastors and other leaders of immigrant Churches. There are doctrinal differences between the mainline Churches and some of the migrant Churches which will probably hold up official recognition for some time. Nevertheless, some recognition should usually be attempted. Simply inviting a pastor of a migrant congregation or fellowship to speak or take part in a service can do this. With further friendship and knowledge, occasional joint services of worship could be arranged.

Many mainline Churches in Europe are only now trying to relate to

63. Steve Chalke, *art. cit,* p. 205.

immigrant Churches that have been on their doorsteps for many years. They are now beginning to understand that 'non-recognition' was a form of racism in that it assumed that European Churches were the 'standard' and others inferior.

Many of the migrant Churches in Ireland are Pentecostal, and most Irish Christians have little knowledge of them. They may even be a little suspicious of strange manifestations and styles of worship. On the other hand, some African Pentecostal Church members regard traditional Irish Churches as being lifeless and lacking what they regard as the manifestations of the Spirit. Allan Anderson and Walter Hollenweger point out that

> Pentecostals are so convinced of the power of their experience that they want to pass it on to everybody... Sometimes they realize that evangelism is a dialogical process in which the evangelists also learn something of the Gospel from the ones they want to evangelise. [64]

In the Irish context there is an opportunity for Pentecostals and Christians of many traditions to enter into a dialogical process, without feelings of superiority on any side, so as to learn from one another.

At national level it is to be hoped that many more of the African Churches will be able to make links with the Irish Council of Churches. One possible way of doing this would be to grant membership in some form to the newly formed Ethnic Minority Christian Leaders Network. This network now has 20-25 immigrant Churches in association. An enlarged Irish Council of Churches could then discuss matters of common interest such as sharing buildings and perhaps find an agreed policy. Full participation in the work of the ICC by immigrant Churches would benefit all.

*Authority*

The authority of Jesus Christ was strong within the early Church. They were also open to the guidance of the Holy Spirit.

The Ephesian Moment of today has this in common with the original Ephesian Moment that the authority of Jesus Christ and the guidance of

64. Allan H. Anderson and Walter J. Hollenweger, *Pentecostals After a Century* (Sheffield, Sheffield Academic Press,1999), p. 190.

the Spirit must be paramount. If we are returning to a situation that is pre-Constantinian some traditions and Church structures built up during the days of Christendom may have to be questioned. Many Christians still feel the close link between their sense of nationhood, their culture and their Church. Yet if we live in cosmopolitan societies with the influence of many cultures we cannot associate the Church exclusively with any one culture as has happened in the past. Instead, all branches of the Church, including new migrant Churches that have come to Ireland and elsewhere, need to strive more diligently to become a counter-culture as the Church was in the early centuries.

If we are living through a new Ephesian Moment, the Church should be engaging in the experiment of finding oneness in the midst of various cultures, ethnicities, and variations of status and generations, this unity being based upon the authority of Jesus Christ and his reconciling work.

*Common Goal*

Churches sharing the same building or operating in the same area should be able to find things to do together. Similarly being members of national inter-church structures can enable the migrant Churches to contribute to common enterprises. It may well be that through the practice of working together with a common goal, theological understanding will improve and there will be mutual enrichment. Common *praxis* may well be a means of producing intercultural theology.

*Other Elements of Reconciliation: Truth*

A member of a trans-cultural local Church when asked what differences of doctrine or practice caused problems in the congregation replied, 'I do not know because we do not spend enough time together to discuss those matters.'[65] The experience granted to us in cosmopolitan cities of meeting together for worship and socializing across cultural boundaries should also be used to seek the truth together. The same applies to meetings at national level between representatives of the older Churches in Ireland and the new Churches and fellowships that have come or grown in recent years.

65. A.C. Varghesi

## Conclusion

This study began with the statement of Janet Schofield that simply putting children and young people of different ethnic/cultural backgrounds together does not ensure positive social outcomes. It seems that she is right. Not only is this true for children and young people; it is true for adults as well. People naturally gravitate to their own cultural, linguistic or regional groups.

Among the first generation of Christians in Ephesus there were initiatives that led to positive social outcomes. Contemporary trans-cultural local Churches in Ireland and the sharing of buildings all required initiative. They also required certain circumstances that brought people into close proximity. Will initiatives be taken to grasp the opportunities presented in a growing number of places throughout the world?

It was people with vision who took the initiative among the Ephesian Christians:

> But now in Christ Jesus you who once were far off have been brought near by the blood of Christ. For he is our peace: in his flesh he has made both groups into one and has broken down the dividing wall, that is, the hostility between us.[66]

To believe such a vision took a huge step of faith. It ran counter to those who saw a world full of permanent 'dividing walls.' To believe such a vision required an interpretation of the life of Jesus that ran counter to those who saw him defeated and discredited. To these Ephesian people of faith, Jesus, who shocked his contemporaries by eating at table with people regarded as 'enemies' and suffered at the hands of those who disapproved, was not defeated but lifted up by God.

There are many people today taking initiatives to remove walls of hostility without the clear vision of the Ephesian Christians but, I believe, with God's approval. Contemporary Christians who consciously come together across social boundaries are doubly significant because they are not only doing something that produces positive social outcome but also bearing witness to God's ultimate purpose for humankind.

66. New Revised Standard Version

# Embracing the Different Other [1]

SAHR YAMBASU

I see in the story of Peter and Cornelius (Acts 10-11) a drama of cross-cultural embrace.[2] It starts with the fact that Cornelius and Peter are separated by geographical, cultural and religious distance: Peter was visiting with a friend in Joppa, Cornelius was living in his home in Caesarea; Peter is a Galilean peasant Jew; Cornelius is Roman Gentile military officer; and Peter is a Christian, Cornelius is a God-fearer.

But both men have at least three things in common: each actively believes in God; each is prayerful; and each receives a vision from God while praying, but at different times.

Cornelius is told in the vision that God has heard his prayers and accepted his gifts to the poor (i.e., his heart and life are in the right place with God). He is told also that he should send and invite Peter. To do what? Cornelius is not told.

The next day Peter sees a vision of a sheet full of clean and unclean animals according to the Law of Moses. He is asked to kill and eat from among the animals. He refuses to do what has been forbidden by his religion and culture. Even when the voice tells him: 'What God has made clean, you must not call unclean' (10:15), he still does not budge.

The content of the vision each man receives is different.Neither man knows the meaning of his vision. This is because each vision is incomplete and will need the other to make complete sense. Each man will have to hear from the other, sharing what God has communicated to him. This would happen only when the men meet face-to-face – an act which will lead these two men, hitherto strangers, to embrace each other as brothers.

In this there is a clear suggestion that cross-cultural embrace is God's

1. This chaper is based on an address delivered at a colloquium on interculturalism at NUI Maynooth, 18 September 2004.

2. I am indebted to Laura B. Lewis, Ronald H. Crann, and James Michael Lee for their insightful interpretation of this story in Barbara Wilkerson (ed.), *Multicultural Religious Education*, Birmingham, 1997, Alabama: Religious Education Press, pp. 330-8

intention for us. The insight we have about life in the world is incomplete by and in it self. To be complete, and to make full sense, the insight needs to be complemented by another insight. This underlines our need for others, their insights, resources, skills, strengths, and experiences, to complement our own.

Cross-cultural Christian embrace is impossible without sharing with one another what God has given and taught us in life. It is through this interdependent learning – this give-and-take relationship – that we are able to know God's will and are supported and helped by others to do it.

## OPENNESS TO THE CULTURAL OTHER

In his book, *Exclusion and Embrace: a Theological Exploration of Identity, Otherness, and Reconciliation*,[3] Miroslav Volf identifies steps in the process of embrace. He describes these steps as: 'opening the arms', 'waiting', 'closing the arms', and 'opening the arms again'.

When we open our arms towards someone, our open arms become a symbol of desire to reach out towards others, a sign that we have created space in ourselves for others to come in and inhabit. In so far as our open arms are a statement that we cannot do without others, they also become an invitation to others to create space in themselves for us to inhabit.

We see this happening in the uninhibited and risky openness on the parts of both Peter and Cornelius towards the different cultural other. This openness takes each of these two men, and those associated with them, on a journey beyond themselves – a journey beyond their incomplete understanding of God's intention for them.

This journey is not easy for either man. In the cultural tradition of Cornelius, an intimate meeting between Jew and Gentile is unusual, to say the least. From Peter's point of view, it is simply against religious law to meet a Gentile. Yet both men are willing to risk crossing cultural boundaries. They do so because they have first embraced God and, so, are ultimately open to God's command and not under the rule of history, tradition, or culture, important as these may be.

This willingness comes about by their doing what God tells them to do. Since he saw his vision before Peter saw his, Cornelius is the one who

3. 1996, Nashville: Abingdon Press, pp. 140-7.

acts first on the incomplete and limited information given him in his vision. He immediately sends two slaves and one of his soldiers to Joppa to find Peter and invite him to his home (Acts 10:7). He also shares his vision with these men, thus translating his private experience into a public narrative. All he has to do now is to wait.

Waiting is what Miroslav Volf identifies as the second step in the movement towards embrace. On the part of the one who waits, waiting is an act of discipline, self-control, and education in patience. It is a statement about our own powerlessness to make people accept us. It is an acknowledgement that we respect others' freedom to agree to relate or not to relate with us. Waiting is not an idle posture. It is a time within which we are afforded the opportunity to woo the other, a time to work towards making the other desire to embrace us.

For the one being waited for, waiting is a statement that the waiter respects your will. It is a statement that the waiter acknowledges and respects your freedom and power to reject, accept, or decide how much to receive or reject of the offer of embrace being made.

Waiting reminds us that embrace is not about forcing others to do our will. It is an act that has to be entirely voluntary if it is to be true.

By sending word to Peter to invite him to his home, Cornelius has initiated the first step towards embracing a stranger. Now he has to wait for the response of Peter – the second necessary step he has to take. Cornelius, being an officer of the occupying power could have chosen to order Peter to come to him. But he did not.

When Cornelius' messengers arrive next day in Joppa, Peter has just received his vision and is wondering what it could mean. He sees no connection between Cornelius' invitation and the meaning of his own vision. Nevertheless, Peter accepts the Spirit's guidance that he should go with Cornelius' messengers. So he accepts Cornelius' invitation.

The question of what to do with three unexpected Gentile visitors is Peter's first real and crucial test of openness towards the cultural other. Should he take the risk of inviting them to stay with him overnight? Or should he let them go and look for a place to stay on their own? Note that Peter takes the cultural risk of inviting them to spend the night in his borrowed lodging.

Cornelius' first move towards embracing a stranger is already being reciprocated by Peter. It is the beginning of Volf's third step in the movement of embrace, what he calls 'closing the arms'. We'll return to this third step below, because actual face-to-face encounter and embrace are yet to come. Yes, what we already seen happening spells hope of a blessed and an enriching encounter.

We should note also that the community that surrounds Cornelius and Peter is growing, as others are included. When Peter travels to Cornelius the next day, he brings with him believers from Joppa who are willing to join him in going to a Gentile's house. Meanwhile, in Caesarea, Cornelius is gathering members of his household and some close friends to await Peter's arrival. Eventually, as the story that started with two men and God unfolds, it draws in the apostles and the Church in Jerusalem. The community of Jews and Gentiles who can worship God together without fear of colour, culture, and creed is being built up: the Kingdom of God is being enlarged.

### FACE-TO-FACE ENCOUNTER

The moment of face-to-face encounter between Peter and Cornelius happens in Acts 10:25. From now on there are no messengers or intermediaries. This is the stage in the drama of embrace that Volf calls 'closing the arms' – the third step towards the movement of embrace. This actual act of embrace is unthinkable without reciprocity. Each must hold the other and must be held by the other in return. It's done gently so that one does not crush the other(s) being held, nor assimilate them. Assimilation is an act of power over another by which the other person(s) are taken into oneself, caused to lose their individuality and identity, and denied the opportunity to exercise power with oneself. It is an act of violence that seeks to nullify the other. Embrace is not about violence.

This is the point in the story when key and complex exchanges happen in this cross-cultural encounter. When Peter and Cornelius meet face-to-face, they engage in what all peoples who meet, engage in: communication, non-verbal and verbal.

The non-verbal communication here is symbolically very powerful. Peter, a Jew, walks into the house of Cornelius, a Gentile, a forbidden space for a Jew. Cornelius, a Roman officer, falls at the feet of Peter, a Galilean peasant. This is an act of obeisance reserved only for divine beings and human authorities of the highest order. It is an unthinkable, perhaps even foolish, act by an officer of an occupying power.

The verbal communication between Peter and Cornelius can be divided into five forms: confession, history lesson, testimony, listening to others, and hospitality.

'Stand up; I am only human' (Acts 10:26) is an admission verging on a confession. This insight is more than what Peter knew before. Peter has now come to the awareness that Cornelius, the Gentile, is as fully human as he is. In recognising this, Peter has now to examine himself closely. He is no better than Cornelius is in God's sight. Both of them are simply men whom God chooses to value equally as human beings and to use for his good purposes. So the two men meet as equals and enter into the house together: two different men, but equal in God's sight.

Second, there is a history lesson. When we meet with others, we tell them our stories of life, reflecting something of our history – our individual histories and the histories of the people and communities that we belong to and that have shaped our lives. The stories we share with each other are also, by implication, stories about what and who we believe others are.

'You are well aware that it is against our law for a Jew to associate with a Gentile or visit ... ' (v.28a). This is how Peter starts his history lesson for Cornelius and his household. It is an acknowledgement and an acceptance of difference, something that is crucially important if we are going to be genuine in embracing other people. The God in whose image we are made is a God of differences and diversity.

Thirdly, there is a testimny: 'God has shown me that I should not call any person impure or unclean ... I now realise how true it is that God does not show favouritism but accepts people from every nation who fear him and do what is right' (28b, 34-35). Peter is sharing a new discovery God has allowed him to make about Cornelius and his household. It is an indication that he has now begun to understand his vision. It is a revelation that urges him to adopt a new way of being for the future. Simply put, it is a testimony of Peter's conversion to Christ.

Fourth, there is a listening to others: 'May I ask why you sent for me?' (29b), Peter asks Cornelius, giving him the opportunity to share his story. So, Cornelius tells the story of his vision to Peter. Then he adds what he believes Peter was meant to come and do, even though there was nothing of the sort in the vision he had: 'So now all of us are here in the presence of God to listen to all that the Lord has commanded you to say' (10:33). This invitation to Peter to speak is crucial because it allows Peter to preach Jesus Christ as Lord of all and to share his experience of him. Peter's speech will unveil the complete meaning of Cornelius' vision to both Cornelius and Peter. For, as Peter preaches Christ crucified and risen, God confirms to Peter and Cornelius that, indeed, God does not discriminate or show partiality: the Holy Spirit falls on the Gentiles 'in the same way' (10:47) she had fallen on the Jewish Christians before. No special treatment, no special cases; exactly what God intends them to learn from their two separate and incomplete visions.

Consequently, the Gentile converts are baptised. There is now no doubt about the meaning of Cornelius' vision by this stage. Neither is there any doubt as to the full meaning of Peter's vision.

Finally, there is hospitality. Remember, Cornelius is the one who first makes the move toward open hospitality by inviting Peter to his home. Peter reciprocates by letting Cornelius' messengers stay with him two days before his face-to-face encounter with Cornelius. Now, the new Gentile Christians ask Peter 'to stay with them for a few days' (10:48) – a powerful way of saying we accept you as our brothers and friends.

The reciprocal hospitality in this drama of embrace of the cultural other suggests hospitality as an essential element of an inter-cultural encounter of any lasting sort. During it and through it the host and guest share more of themselves with each other and so get to know and accept each other better. Hospitality is a statement of trust and love. Not surprisingly, it is this practice of cross-cultural hospitality and sharing meals that becomes the one big source of challenge and conflict when the news gets back to the Church in Jerusalem: 'When Peter went up to Jerusalem, the circumcised believers criticised him and said, "You went into the house of uncircumcised men and ate with them".' (Acts 11:2-3)

### MOVING FORWARD

The invitation of the new Gentile converts to Peter to stay with them 'for a few days'(10:48b) signals the time for parting is near. It signals what Volf identifies as the fourth and final step in the process of embrace: 'Opening the arms again.'

Brought together by God to share their different and incomplete visions and perspectives, both understand what God wishes them to learn. Now they must part. Peter and his men have to return to where they belong and Cornelius and his people have to stay at home: 'opening arms again'. Embrace does not make two inseparable bodies. If it does, it gets rid of the 'I' and turns it into 'we'. When that happens the ones we embrace are lost in transition. That is what totalitarian regimes are about. That is what some cultural movements and family relationships are like. They aim at making others in their own image rather than helping them be themselves. Yet the embrace leaves those who engage in it no longer the same people they were before the embrace.

Spiritually and culturally, we see that Peter has come quite a distance: from praying on a rooftop in Joppa waiting for a proper, *kosher* Jewish meal to eating in the home of a Roman officer – a Gentile – with newly baptised Gentile believers. This is a remarkable journey of cross-cultural embrace. And one would expect a similar journey for the other Jewish believers who followed him. The same is true for Cornelius too. He has travelled from being a total stranger to Peter and a mere God-fearer to becoming Peter's brother in Christ and Peter's host. The same is true for his friends and members of his household.

Consequently, this drama of the conversion of the first Gentiles to Christianity also becomes a drama about the conversion of the Church as well. In fact, in this narrative of Luke, Peter and company (the insiders and citizens) undergo a change that was perhaps more wrenching by far than the change experienced by Cornelius, his household, and friends.

All of this was possible because God was at the heart of it. I pray that we would allow God in Christ to steer the wheel of our journey of intercultural and inter-racial embrace in Ireland.

# Experiencing Transculturalism

TONY WALSH

Those working at the grass roots in any project have a range of wisdom that often remains unrecognised and untapped. It appeared important to redress this common imbalance and to express something of the experience and views of those most involved in transcultural experiences. In order to connect with something of this richness a group of members involved in transcultural congregations were invited to respond to six questions about their Church's story of multicultural development.

The respondents were selected for the range and depth of their experience in the field as well as for the variety of their cultural backgrounds. Some of the respondents were ministers or leaders, others described themselves as ordinary local Church members. The congregations in which they were involved reflected many differences, coming from a variety of denominational backgrounds and were located in a wide range of differing contexts. All were situated in Ireland, some in urban or suburban areas, others in towns or villages, scattered throughout the country

This chapter tries to encapsulate the respondents' reactions in a way which honours their experience. As well as giving a 'voice' to those most deeply involved in this area of transcultural development, it also seemed imperative to reflect the wide variety of views expressed as well as to note commonality of thought and experience where this existed.

Not all those invited to respond did so, and of those who did, not all answered each question. Responses are, however, characterised by a remarkable degree of reflectiveness and insight. Many are profoundly challenging of the respondents themselves and indicate a very high level of both personal awareness and honesty. A number of responses are also quite challenging of the Church structures and of the larger denominational systems. Some question sensitive issues such as existing structures of power, leadership and tradition. Others share very personal aspects of their own journey. All speak for themselves; their views are not necessarily those of others in their congregation or their denomination. Instead, they are stories of a story. If there is an emergent common theme it may be to suggest that the creation of transcultural community provokes a questioning of the assumed status quo in all sorts of unexpected and frequently uncomfortable ways.

To preserve a sense of privacy for both respondents and the congregations involved, responses are not credited to particular individuals or congregations.

## 1. *In what significant ways has your church changed?*

Some respondents spoke with obvious delight of significant positive alterations in their Church. Others commented on attitudinal changes and one or two mentioned difficulties encountered.

Almost all the respondents noted such obvious transformations as a significant, at times amazing, growth in numbers attending services. Many also described a spectacular increase in the range of cultural backgrounds involved, noting that one new group attending seemed to serve as a catalyst for the involvement of other groups as well:

> We have seen a dramatic increase in numbers as different groups have joined the congregation: local families of different church backgrounds and then asylum seekers, refugees and immigrants – from eight different countries and four continents: Africa, USA, Asia, Europe.

Significant change was also reported in the conduct of worship, with services becoming livelier, more varied musically and much more participative.

> … a cross cultural group of vocalists now leads the singing accompanied by a music ensemble with guitars, African drums, key board and organ.

> We always have Bible readings in a number of languages, and a time of open prayer at every service, so that people can participate in their own way and in their own tongues.

> It was felt really important from the outset that people would be able to understand the message, so it is always translated either directly, or

through power-point headings into two or three other languages.

Most respondents also commented on real attitudinal change as members became more open to embracing difference of any kind. Some also instanced what appeared to be a new willingness to enter into deeper levels of relationship; this frequently accompanied the increasing informality of worship:

> There is... a definite qualitative change. Oh... the church has become much more open to new ideas, to difference; different ways of worshipping, different ways of doing things. People are much more ready to try new experiences of prayer and fellowship.

> New members from different cultures have stimulated friendliness, respect, hospitality, and integration. Worship has become brighter with a time for praise songs in different languages becoming an integral part of each service. Now people will talk together about new ideas and possibilities; not that they'll always agree with everything that's proposed, but they're very willing to discuss and to give things a try.

> People are trying new ways of being a community; talking, spending time, connecting. We often have communal meals together. And prayer in small groups; many services now also include a time of testimony and sharing.

In some instances this openness appears to have occurred right from the beginnings of the multicultural experience, almost as if a congregation was poised, awaiting a catalyst to provoke change. In other situations it took a little more time as original members (and perhaps newcomers) dealt with an initial period of uncertainty and fear. At times it appears that this process involved learning to challenge deeply held assumptions about the role of church.

> At the beginning it was all a bit scary, it was facing the unknown, and people were afraid and unsure.

> The stimulus to outreach and to growth is vital for a healthy congregation. And the recognition that the church must not become a club, inward looking, exclusive, afraid of change or of attempting ventures

in faith. This has meant a strengthening of the original Wesleyan ethos – of an evangelical, evangelistic church.

Unfortunately for many people, I think that the church unwittingly fulfils the function of a bastion against change. It's a place they retreat to, to comfort themselves. In reality it should be a place in which to grow, to be challenged and to take steps of faith.

Posing a question about change can not only provide interesting descriptive information; it can also unearth something of a congregation's core sense of identity, revealing much about how it views itself, it role and its function in the wider society. How an individual or a congregation deals with change is linked to the conscious or unconscious assumptions which they hold about *their* church or about church in general. Sometimes in a rapidly changing society, a church is valued as the one place that is stable and unchanging. Moreover, it may be perceived by some as a place which by its very nature *should* not change. Obviously such deeply held and often largely unconscious assumptive models will be significant, either precluding any major changes or allowing them only at a very modest rate and with considerable resistance. More dynamic assumptive models which accept change and challenge as part of the very essence of church life will allow for a much more ready ability to adapt. The power of these assumptions often resides in the fact that they are largely invisible and therefore are difficult to 'flush out' or reveal let alone challenge.

Even in congregations or indeed denominations where 'bastion' or 'retreat' are strongly underlying metaphors the advent of cultural diversity can over time allow for the transformation of old assumptions. This can allow for their replacement by new and more dynamic models and the concomitant emergence of an array of possibilities.

### 2. *What for you has constituted the most enriching aspects of becoming a transcultural congregation?*

The term 'enrichment' is often used to describe the experience of cultural diversity; of course the precise definition of this experience depends very much on the beholder. Sometimes it implies satisfaction, sometimes challenge; often both. In the second question participants were asked to reflect on this aspect of their congregation's experience.

The excitement of developing a completely new range of cross cultural relationships, individually and as community was one highly significant area commented on by a number of the respondents:

> For me the most exiting part has been meeting so many people from all over the world and the process of getting to know people, so that strangers become friends.

> It is seeing two communities coming together, particularly when they're sharing together and seeing each others' culture. For instance, seeing Irish people choosing to sing in your language [Lingala], a language that is foreign to them, it shows how much they want to share with you.

> It is seeing people open the heart's door: that's the first sign of seeing people wanting to know you; the second step is seeing them listen to you; the third step is them telling you about themselves. Then you really begin to know who they are. Then you can start working together.

Others speak of how their faith has been stretched. Many Irish respondents speak of how the commitment of those coming from other cultures has excited and challenged them at a spiritual level.

> Look at what they've been through and they're still praising God. Their trust, and a times their serenity, in the face of so many past and present difficulties is so amazing.

> They're not ashamed to share Jesus, like we sometimes are.

And the experience of enrichment seems to be mutual as newcomers comment on the spirituality of some Irish believers:

> They have a quiet faith; they do not shout, but if people in Africa believed and behaved like these Irish believers then the problems there would just go away.

> At first because they do not smile so much when they pray, and look sad when they sing those old hymns, you think 'What is this?' But then…then, they show you Jesus, as they open their hearts and doors

and invite you in.

Human beings tend towards being creatures of habit. Organisations of any kind, including Churches, tend, when left to themselves, to avoid change. Encountering different views or practices will often disturb this tendency. Several, particularly those involved in leadership or pastoral roles, speak of the stimulation of having their accustomed understandings and ways of seeing or reacting stretched; of having their minds and imaginations broadened.

> I'd come from a fairly predictable evangelical church background; I needed to be challenged, to be moved out of my own framework to a wider view of things. My view and experience of God has been broadened.
>
> So many of those who have joined us are so warm and open. I think as Irish people we can be very guarded; friendly on the outside, but very guarded beneath that friendly façade.
>
> The experience has challenged us as a church to examine ourselves, to think outside the box and to move beyond the comfort zones in lots of ways.
>
> I think that the most rewarding and exciting aspect is being in the midst of difference and change. It stimulates you to creativity and resourcefulness. You are required to be resourceful in all sorts of unexpected ways. To find resources in yourselves. And in your experience of God.
>
> You learn to expect the unexpected and it's challenging; It's been a very refreshing process; more positive than negative – but definitely not easy.
>
> For years, at an implicit level I think we've questioned our relevance to the wider society. The countryside is littered with derelict Protestant churches; the death of the communities which they represented doesn't seem to have made one whit of difference to Irish life. This can eat away at a community's confidence and make for a very demoralised outlook. I think many of the culturally diverse congregations have shifted significantly in this regard and are looking at themselves

> anew. They're suddenly realising that they have something unique and valuable at their core that has allowed things to develop so amazingly.This creates a new sense of confidence.

Respondents continually use such adjectives as 'refreshing,' 'positive,' and 'rewarding', simultaneously reflecting that the process of transcultural development has been 'stretching' and 'far from easy'.

It is probably true to suggest that many congregations, particularly those of a minority status, tend to live out a rather sheltered and sequestered existence with little that speaks of a radical perspective. While they offer a strong and cohesive sense of community, concerns may become small and perceptions inward looking. This inexorably results in a diminution of confidence and an accompanying underawareness of what they might have to offer to the wider society.

However, where they are able to respond positively to the stimulus of influx and the attendant new ideas, this seems to result in a new elasticity of thought and response at a variety of levels. Over time when a community responds positively and continually to such stimuli, the whole internal culture shifts, becoming more open, inclusive and flexible. What at first may be disconcerting results in the expansion of existing understandings and the growth of more elastic constructions of reality. The resultant sense of confidence is bolstered as they uncover something of their own latent resources. This is further reinforced as they are recognised as doing something novel, dynamic and useful by the wider community and indeed at times by society at large. It would appear that for those congregations involved in an engagement with transculturalism the experience is simultaneously enriching and extending, as well as being an invitation to revisit their own sense of worth.

### 3. *What did you find most challenging in the process?*

All the participants suggested that the process of transcultural development had faced them with significant challenges. They noted that such challenges existed primarily at two levels. A number of respondents discovered that real engagement with profound cultural difference was deeply disconcerting, inviting them to levels of reflection and learning that were both difficult and unexpected. Secondly, many found themselves profoundly challenged to reflect critically on their accustomed ways of being, and of their understanding of their own role in the church. They confronted unexpected closed areas in their own thought or behaviour patterns, or suddenly recognised an inappropriate attachment to power or control in the fulfilment of leadership or other functions.

Recognising that different behaviours or assumptions, including many of ones own, are culturally determined rather than necessarily right or wrong, can be highly disconcerting, but can also result in the need to radically revise accustomed outlooks in order to fit with this new realisation. It may also invite quite profound shifts in thinking and behaviour in order to allow for more comfortable fit with those of other cultures.

> Misunderstanding of our behaviour was perhaps hardest. Sometimes you don't think about cultural difference until you hit against it. For instance in our culture we never invite true friends to visit. They do not need an invitation, your home is theirs and you just expect them to call. Irish friends didn't understand this and thought they were not welcome because they were not invited. And we began to think they did not want to come, because they did not call.

> When you experience a certain reaction or behaviour that is unexpected you have to learn to think 'Well now what might that mean in another culture?' rather than jumping to negative conclusions. You also have to be really aware of how what you do or say may be interpreted in another culture. Actually at one stage I became quite paralysed, a bit paranoid really, afraid to do anything. But then I learned to say 'I don't understand what this means,' and to ask for feedback about what I was doing, if I felt unsure. I think we've got into the habit now of asking and discussing, and of clarifying the meaning of behaviour a lot more, and that really helps.

> Encountering Irish people in churches, you find that many are ready to meet and invite; but not everyone coming into the new community is ready to step forward to meet them. Many newcomers are not making a step to meet half way which would make it much easier; many in their hearts are not really committing to the new community. At the beginning you sit, then when you see people are willing to open their heart, then you should stand up and take responsibility. Many new-

> comers do not do this. They never consider how will my attitude, my behaviour appear to those of another culture, an Irish culture?
>
> We have been brought up to think that the way we prioritise, legislate behave and believe is the best, if not the only valid way to see and do. If you really meet the other person of another culture, you have to be open to questioning all that. It can leave you feeling quite rudderless and uncertain.'
>
> Helping some older members to face their own unexpected and unsuspected tendency towards racism was particularly challenging…for everyone.

For some there was a new awareness of how the *way* in which they occupied their role in the church could either facilitate or block growth; this highlighted the issue of power and control in local congregations. One or two reflected very courageously on their tendency to hold on to control, by preventing change or by adopting a directive rather than a facilitative style of leadership.

> What shocked me, as a minister, was not the challenges encountered in transculturalism but my own reactions: being intolerant, holding on to the familiar, trying to maintain control…..This has been very challenging for me personally; ministers are very invested in maintaining control. Some of it comes from the training and maybe some of it is due to the personality types that are selected for ministry. I have had to put a lot of work into learning to be more open, more flexible; to shifting my comfort levels, to let go of control. Because if you don't, if you're not genuinely open, you will find yourself constantly on the defensive and consequently you will create problems, stifle good ideas and prevent growth.
>
> Becoming a minister who is a facilitator of the growth of others, of their ideas and of their roles, is much more difficult than occupying the traditional role of minister-as-boss.

Another leader very honestly acknowledged:

> We can believe things quite erroneously about ourselves; for instance we can believe ourselves to be very open to change and development,

> but when it comes down to the practice of this openness in a new situation, it is much more difficult. At times in the past I know I presented a façade of openness. But it was a façade. The process of transculturalism has challenged me most profoundly. It has made me look at myself as never before. I now know how closed I can sometimes be.

Religion and identity can be very closely aligned. For members of Irish churches, particularly perhaps the minority churches, congregational affiliation is often not just about spirituality, or even about a social network. It can be experienced as core to people's very identity. Their position or locus of influence in a local church as a result can become very, very important. Change, particularly radical change which may endanger this can be perceived as highly threatening.

> Life can revolve around the church. For some people it's the centre not just of their spiritual life but of their social world as well. If they've put in years keeping things going, it can be very, very difficult for them to let go. Because this may mean letting go of their influence, or of the roles that keep them going.

> I sometimes watch Mrs.H.....; she's a widow and her family are all long gone. She used to play the old pipe organ we had, and could coax music out of it in a way no one else could. Everyone knew her even in the wider community as the organist in that little Protestant church. Now we've an intercultural praise band and she sits at the back by herself. While the church has gained immeasurably by the changes, I think she has lost out so much. No wonder she wasn't too keen on the new people.

It appears that many congregations now developing into transcultural churches gradually drifted into the area. People of different cultures arrived and the congregation responded without necessarily having a clear idea of what might be implied in terms of change and adaptation. Perhaps few of the newcomers realised this either. The reality that close contact with another culture might imply having to review one's own assumptions and values as well as normative ways of doing things may not have been recognised until the encounter was well under way. It is also doubtful if many realised that they could find themselves projected into an arena where they were confronted by their own prejudices. Where there has been opposition to cultural diversity, this can have its roots not so much in racism or prejudice, but in the fear of loosing influence, control or security.

Those congregations who have even at an unconscious level decided to remain disengaged from multiculturalism, or those individuals or groups who have opted to join churches of their own ethnic origin may have almost inadvertently shielded themselves from the rigours of the challenges embedded in the experience of transculturalism.

### 4. *Were there particular events, moments or experiences that were of seminal importance in the experience of transcultural development?*

In a process of change and growth there will frequently be particular events or experiences which are of seminal importance in the development of a project. Sometimes these are actual crossroads, where one direction is taken rather than another and this has made all the difference. Sometimes there are moments of reflection or discovery when scales fall from the eyes of those involved and they see in a new way. Occasionally a particular event or moment can attain a symbolic significance and progress is measured from that time; it assumes a central place in the narrative of a community's development. In recognition of this the next question invited respondents to reflect on such moments in the life of their church. In response some chose particular events which were in some way significant while others focused on particular moments which had promoted insight or had altered thinking in a significant way.

> It may be strange to choose a row as a special moment, but it was such a revelation. Two groups from another culture had a major difference one Sunday. It was very public and very loud. People were so ashamed afterwards, they felt so humiliated. One family could never bring themselves to come back. I don't think that I had ever acknowledged before how vulnerable it can feel to be in a minority culture, although I've been part of one all my life. The whole thing made me so much more aware of lots of barely acknowledged issues within my

own life. That in turn alerted me to what may be issues for those in other minority communities in our new Ireland.

There were so many really significant moments. Some of these were very important, symbolically. When two Africans were married the reception was held in an Irish home. That showed the true love that was extended in our community at a time of celebration and excitement. ... Other special times were when Bill and Doreen (Irish members) invited us to their house to a barbecue and again when the whole congregation met together in a house to welcome the new pastor and to eat together. When you are invited to a home then you know the heart is truly being opened to you. It is one thing to worship together; that may be easy. It is when doors of homes and hearts are also open, then change really takes place.

A Nigerian family who had been with us for a while decided to make a family birthday into a church event. They cooked all the food, brought it to the church and invited everyone to stay and celebrate with them. It was a wonderful occasion; Irish members had never thought of anything like that before. Now we have quarterly meals together after the morning service; everyone brings food to share and it's a great opportunity for getting to know people and for strengthening relationships'.

These last two respondents are underlining the importance not just of the abstract concept of Christian love, but of love that is grounded in the actuality of invitation, where the normative societal boundaries are superseded. Irish culture is noted for its warmth; in reality this friendliness can at times be limited to the pub or other external spaces. Opening homes or inviting the community to become part of a family celebration are powerful symbolic gestures that go far beyond the usual norms. The stranger is invited into the inner life and reality of the host rather than being kept at a safer social distance. This can feel quite a risky undertaking, particularly at first, as the hosts are rendered vulnerable to the gaze and judgement of the outsider and indeed to the possibility of rejection or refusal.

The importance of initiative is also being underlined here, and the recognition of how one courageous gesture can create a precedent leading to a greatly enriched community life.

Once we made trip all together [to Glendalough], to see something of the Irish culture and countryside. Some people had never been outside Dublin before, and we all felt 'Oh they're showing us not just love but something that is important to them, they want us to know more about their life, their history, what is important to them.'

Since the start we had a Christmas party every year for the newcomers, with a special meal involved. The third Christmas that the Congolese group were with us they suggested that they would cook the meal. We sampled all these exotic foods that are part of a Congolese way of life, the Chorale sang, and there was lots of chat and fun. Everyone still talks about it. But it wasn't just the event, though that was great. For the first time our African friends were able to show us, involve us in something of their culture. And for a change, perhaps for the first time since they came to Ireland, they were able to be hosts. The balance was being redressed.

Starting the special African style prayer meetings, when everyone met together in homes to pray as we do at home, to share with us in our way, was a big milestone. You knew that people really wanted to come and share as well as to pray together; and everyone was making a very special effort to attend to share our spirituality. It says we are a family learning together from each other's differences.

Starting a praise group was definitely one of the most important developments. There are more than a dozen people involved in it at present, Malaysian, Korean, Nigerian, Congolese, Irish. They use keyboard, drums, konga, piano, guitar as well as vocalists. The group meets every Saturday to practise so they get to know each other really well and have become a very rich intercultural sub-system. They lead at all the services and this has really transformed the worship. It also allows for the inclusion of very different styles of music and praise and is a way of allowing different cultures to share their richness and their particular spirituality in worship. And it allows a much larger and more culturally diverse group to develop and share their talents as well as facilitating more people to actively participate in visible leadership.

We used to have a very stable membership. This seems to be changing. People come and go a lot more now, arriving and spending some time and then moving on in God's providence to take up other roles for Him in different places. I think we're realising that church life may be altering dramatically, becoming less predictable and more varied. People will be with us for a while, sharing with us and we with them, and then they'll move on to other places. Its an invitation to draw on the gifts of a much wider group. God's telling us to look at the bigger picture. I think that this calls for more faith on our part; firstly to trust that He will provide the people and the resources to run the church and secondly to trust the wisdom and experience of those who come in from different cultures. Up to recently I suspect we have probably relied far too heavily on the predictability of our own resources. This moment of realisation has been a real eye opener.

These commentators underline the value of occasions when there are real 'meetings', which go beyond mere surface connection. Perhaps more significantly they underline the importance of an open invitational attitude of mind. They also emphasise the importance of occasions where those who are in a marginal position in the new society are offered, or empower themselves to find, a context in which to demonstrate the wealth of their culture and spirituality. This emphasises the need to be aware of the temptation to see the newcomers as primarily 'refugees' with many needs, rather than as people who have a wealth of resources to share. A central role of the transcultural congregation is not just to privilege participation it is also to find creative ways in which members of different cultures can express and share the wealth of their experience.

### 5. *Do you feel that your thinking has changed in response to transculturalism?*

As responses to previous questions have indicated, building trans-cultural community constitutes a constant stimulus to new learning. In reflecting on their experience many of the respondents were able to identify quite fluently how this new learning had impacted on their thought processes. Some indicated a change in the quality of their thinking; in the past they would have been less able, or less willing perhaps, to question or critique.

I think that after a while you begin not just to do a little differently but to think quite differently too. We are so used to our society, our church structures, our accustomed ways of doing things, that we rarely pause to question or critique them at any depth. Are these really the best or most valid ways of proceeding? Do they really serve and advance the Lord's work? We rarely try to get beneath our practices or structures to look at what's embedded there. So much of what we do in churches is about preserving our comfort zones and not challenging the status quo. Its also about preserving sites of power. So many of our committees, rituals, offices and assemblies are about preserving the power and status of the denominational structure, or the elders or the clergy rather than about trying to follow Jesus effectively. Most particularly, much of it's about preserving a very Eurocentric value system which privileges individuality, success and certainty.

Because we're so used to the assumptions that are involved we're inclined to accept things 'as they are' without any real question. In fact things are 'as they are' because our society or our church has chosen to construct its world and its priorities in a particular way. We need to be aware that there are always other choices, there are always different ways of doing things or of seeing things. Real transcultural engagement challenges us to realise that there are so many different but equally valid ways of viewing reality, of prioritising, of doing things. It's not to say that other ways of doing or seeing are always better than what we're accustomed to. That's not the point at all. Rather it's to say there are different possibilities that invite us to question, to re-evaluate and perhaps then to re-create. I sometimes wonder if interculturalism gets only vague support from the main church bodies and tends to exist more at the margins because it is, almost unconsciously, perceived as in some way threatening to the denominational status quo.

Our church hasn't changed much despite all the newcomers, despite our lip service to inclusiveness. It seems that the real issue is that we have continued as on the basis that 'they' are welcome to join 'us'. There are two real problems here as I see it; the first is about control, and particularly about who maintains control, particularly control of the content of the service. The second is about creating purely tokenistic change which is more cosmetic than real. This preserves the status quo by keeping those in power happy; those without power continue to be excluded in any real way, but appearances of 'doing the decent thing' are maintained. The main problem is not about multiculturalism; it is located in the reaction to it.

Our society is so rushed and so focused on doing rather than being that it's easy to forget that the core building blocks of relationship and Christian fellowship are actually quite simple. Difficult but simple! The first is the priority of listening. Its only if we listen carefully, caringly and non-judgementally that we will learn about the other – whoever they are. The second is the importance of discussing and dialoguing continuously. If people are continually involved in both formal and informal processes of discussion it is much harder for difficulties to become 'solidified'. There will always be different attitudes and expectations, particularly when you're dealing with people from different cultures. Getting these out in the open, exploring them openly, often helps people to shift, or at least to understand the position of the other, and if people understand then they can often move. With either listening or discussing the problem is time. Both take inordinate amounts of time, but they're very worthwhile.

We as people coming in from other countries should have more commitment to show what we can do, or who we can be in the community. Often we are not saying or showing what we can do. We have entered the house, eaten the meal and now we just sit down. Sometimes for those who come in to a church they are afraid to suggest, or are not suggesting. Often because back home we are used to accepting the minister or priest as the authority figure…we only do things if they tell you what to do. They are never, ever challenged. So it becomes a habit not to express a view or opinion; to say everything is o.k. when it is not. If something goes wrong in the church then, you can blame without having to take responsibility.

New learning not only results in new behaviours; it also frequently creates radical and sometimes unexpected changes in pre-existing outlooks. What was in the past accepted as normal can suddenly be opened to critique and questioning. Contact with people from other cultures can ultimately promote a radical questioning of accepted norms and structures in one's own society or community of faith. Perhaps this is one of the more unexpected results of openness to cultural diversity.

While being greatly enriching, this shift does not necessarily guarantee a comfortable fit with the status quo, societal or denominational. This may well have long-term implications for how transcultural congregations are perceived by both. And in turn this will tend to be of significance in defining how their evolving needs are met. It is interesting to note that the Waldensians, the small but influential indigenous Protestant church of Italy, are considering a radical re-vamping of their ministerial training programme in order to address multicultural issues.

### 6. *What do you see as important for the future?*

Finally, respondents were asked to comment on future plans based on what they had learned in the evolving process of developing a transcultural community. Much of what was shared was very practical. Looking to the future the importance of partnership and participation was emphasised again and again as was the need to involve women in the development of strong, culturally diverse local leadership.

> It seems very important in the context of an intercultural congregation to develop a strong non-Irish leadership to have input into decision making and particularly to have a significant voice in the future development of the church. So far while three African members have been elected to the church council their attendance at meetings and their contribution to discussion has been very disappointing. I'm not sure how we can change this and encourage the development of really meaningful and active Christian leadership in this context. Perhaps when people become more settled in Ireland, and are guaranteed that their future is secure here, they may feel more able to contribute more realistically. A second issue is the development of a number of home fellowship groups, meeting in the different areas of our small city. These would nurture participation and help people to grow spiritually and in cross-cultural relationship. They might also with time aid the development of leadership skills and responsibility.

> Women's place and role within the church is traditionally limited. While this is changing, I'm not sure that It's changing either fast enough or meaningfully enough. There is a huge need to validate and value women's ways of knowing and doing and to utilise their leadership skills. Of course, in the context of interculturalism this is something of an issue, as many of the new cultures now in Ireland have an even more patriarchal and paternalistic attitude to women than that of Irish churches.

> To work more with women. On the surface it seems that in many societies women have small roles. This is not true. For us women are the ones who really push; they are the strong ones.

> Invite the suggestions of new-comers; go to the fields, harvest the opinions, views, suggestions...and their contributions. Ask 'What do you think we should do...what would you be willing to do?...what would help?' This starts people to think, it involves them. Many people from Africa are not used to thinking, to being asked for their opinion on church, only gradually will they learn to change, to realise that their view is valued. Only then will they become responsible. The pastor, the leaders should not just visit, they must consult, discuss, feedback and discuss again.

Responses also emphasised the profoundly fulfilling nature of transcultural development but did not shrink from recognising the difficulties involved. They emphasised the need to be tentative rather than prescriptive, to experiment and to risk rather than being tied to rigid plans or to traditional approaches.

# Changing Culture

TONY WALSH

There are outsiders always. These stars –
These iron inklings of an Irish January,
Whose light happened
Thousands of years before
Our pain did: they are, they always have been
Outside history.
Eavan Boland (1944- )

Culture, change and learning are recurring topics in transcultural development. This chapter uses material drawn from theorists, in conjunction with quotations from those who took part in interviews about the the experience of transcultural congregations,[1] to explore these areas.

Travellers to other countries when entering into a real engagement with the cultures they meet abroad, often report themselves profoundly changed by such encounters. Similarly, those involved in developing transcultural community, experience comparable transformations as they enter co-operative relationships with those of other cultures. Previously existing world views, meaning systems and accustomed behaviours experience challenge, often resulting in the development of new ways of seeing and inhabiting the world. Interviews with people involved in transcultural communities display a sense of enthusiasm and excitement, with moments also of challenge and frustration. At the core of their comments lies a conviction that transcultural development is not a process of newcomers adapting to a Eurocentric cultural milieu, or a melting pot where difference is reduced to the lowest common denominator. Instead, it is about the creation of something much more radical: a new way of being community where difference is both acknowledged and honoured. In this exciting and challenging process an awareness of what consti-

1. Quotations from interviews with people involved in transcultural congregations are printed in italics within a box.

tutes cultural difference, an understanding of how people and groups negotiate change and a sensitivity to the potential and difficulties involved in new learning are important topics for exploration.

Cultural difference implies far more than a different language and some unexpected behaviours; at a much more radical level it can entail a completely different understanding of the world, and a totally different range of assumptions about ethics, relationships and priorities. When individuals from ethnically or nationally disparate backgrounds are working together towards developing common goals, an understanding of what is embedded within the idea of *culture,* and of how *cultural difference* operates can be of great assistance.

In a different but related context, every group or organisation, irrespective of its ethnic background or location, has its own particular subculture or collection of mindsets which are separate from but not unrelated to the wider cultural milieu in which the organisation exists. The idea of culture is also useful in teasing out the elements of these microclimates which largely dictate the ways of thinking, the accepted behaviours and the vision for future development which exist within any group.

Operating with a transcultural agenda invites a sensitivity to and an understanding of culture at both these levels.

Secondly there are a number of stages and a range of tasks involved in the evolution of transcultural community. While these may vary from context to context, interviews wirth members of transcultural communities suggest that they tend to imply varying levels of *change* for all those most closely involved. Consequently it is important to be aware of the dynamics of change, what it implies and how people tend to respond to it. This in turn invites a consideration of how best to support and facilitate the change process for individuals as well as for communities.

Lastly, a number of those interviewed referred to the amount of new *learning* involved in transcultural endeavour. Consequently an appreciation of the nature and process of learning seems important for those involved in the development of transcultural community.

This chapter explores aspects of these areas by drawing on the disciplines of cultural studies, change management, organisational studies and learning theory to offer some ideas which may be of use to transcultural congregations and others involved in similar work. A greater understanding of issues which they are likely to arise, or may already have arisem can prove a useful resource in anticipating or resolving some of the difficulties which are part of any creative enterprise. Having a fresh awareness of both the resources as well as the pitfalls can facilitate more realistic strategic planning for any development project. One person involved in a transcultural congregation pointed out: 'Develop loose and fluid structures that support what's happening rather than clinging to those you've inherited from the past or from the denomination. If something isn't working ditch it'.

## CULTURE

> *It's only if we listen carefully, caringly and non-judgementally that we will learn about the other. This is particularly so when dealing with people of a different culture. It's only through really hearing their stories and experiences and their values that you can begin to...get some sense of their culture, their world of beliefs and assumptions.*

As already suggested, the concept of culture can be addressed in two particular ways. The first involves considering the notion at a macro level where it is seen as a framework through which to explore the differing values, customs and ways of making sense of the world which distinguish one national or ethnic group or tribe from another. Every national or tribal group has a particular range of behaviours, meanings and priorities that make it different from other groups. These understandings and reactions are core to how it manages both its internal and external relationships. They includes a group's unique, shared ways of making sense of the world and their ways of interpreting the meanings of life and death.

Coming to an accurate understanding of such nuanced and often slippery assumptive worlds and ways of making meaning is not easy. Yet gaining some kind of a map of how different peoples think, react and prioritise is vital to creating understanding and co-operation between two or more groups coming from different ethnic backgrounds. At a practical level in transcultural endeavours it is important to understand why another cultural group may behave in a particular way, and to understand the range of meanings that this behaviour implies. It is of course equally important for incomers to become aware of the host country's culturally defined behaviours and reactions and what these may mean.

Observers will often comment on the startling differences which exist between congregations or sub-groups despite their coming from similar social and denominational backgrounds. They comment on differing levels of friendliness, creativity, conservatism or liberalism, spontaneity or formalism as well as the quality and degree of connection with the wider community. The term 'culture' can also be used at this more localised, or micro level, to describe the internal climate or the shared mental models which characterise such a community. This climate shapes and influences the behaviours and priorities of the group and its members along certain lines. It also informs the groups' sense of its own role, identity and purpose. Exploring the concept of congregational culture will often explain why a particular avenue of development will be welcomed by one community and shunned by another, or why a new proposal may be welcomed by one and given short shrift by another.

*We were at an African birthday party; it seemed very familiar to anyone Irish; all the women were in the kitchen and all the men in the front room. They were chatting together and the young boys were in a separate group at the back of the room. During a pause in the conversation, unusual at any African social event, (I think everyone was a bit worn out from the strain of translating into English for my benefit), you could hear all these little African lads talking about football, and their teams. But it was GAA they were talking and in strong Dublin accents. You could sense a sudden change in the quality of the men's silence, and in their faces as they listened to their sons' conversation. There was a huge pause in that room; it was as though the world stood still. For me it felt like trespassing on a moment of revelation. Through it I had a dramatic encounter with what it means to loose your culture.*

*I think out of the blue those men were faced, in a very stark way with the reality that whatever happened, their sons could never be African in the way that they themselves were.*

*Sometimes for better or worse there is no going back.*

*Macro-cultures*

We frequently use the word 'culture' as being limited to such pursuits as art, music and literature. It is much more useful, and more accurate to suggest that culture is a socially constructed range of lenses through which members of a society learn to interpret and respond to the events around them. Members of any particular cultural group, largely unconsciously, buy into this set of lenses which organise and to a large extent dictate their assumptions, values and behaviours. Colin Lago notes:

> Culture is socially transmitted and profoundly affects our ways of seeing and thinking about the world, of understanding relationships among people, things and events, of establishing preferences and purposes, and of carrying out actions and pursuing goals.[2]

The central structures of any society, its political and educational institutions, legal and religious establishments and its family structures have a significant role to play in reinforcing these powerful norms. Frequently, members of a culture are unaware of the actual practices through which they are socialised into a particular set of norms. The process is often so successful that those who share the same cultural background tend to assume unquestioningly their particular range of beliefs and behaviours are the 'only' way, at very least the 'best' way of viewing reality or of living life. Frequently, they are unaware of the power of the constraints under which they operate. Often it is only in meeting with members of a very different culture that people begin to compare and question, and ultimately to recognise the particular range of assumptions and behaviours which comprise the bedrocks of their own culture.

Any society schools its members to emphasise particular values and underplay others. Certain ways of thinking, certain ways of interpreting events and situations are seen as valid; others are not. Actions and behaviours flow from these powerful filters. Such aspects of culture exist at a number of levels, some of which are conscious, others unconscious; some clear, visible and explicit, others more hidden and implicit.

Language, customs, social rituals around birth, marriage or death, history and folklore are easy enough to observe. We may experience these as variously fascinating, mysterious or just plain inconvenient. The greater problem tends to occur however with those aspects of culture which are less visible. These include verbal and non-verbal communica-

2. Colin Lago, *Race, Counselling and Culture,* 1996, Buckingham: Open University Press, p. 33.

tion style, ordering of priorities, role expectations and definition of efficiency. For instance, a small Nigerian boy, being upbraided for poor homework in a Dublin school met the overworked teacher's onslaught with silence and downcast eyes. Later, in describing the incident the teacher defined the child as not only disobedient and troublesome (because of the lack of homework) but also as sullen and shifty. 'He went into a sulk; he couldn't even meet my eyes.' The small boy was in fact acting with utmost politeness according to the dictates of his home culture. He had been taught the rudeness of ever making eye-to-eye contact or of justifying himself to any authority figure. Both pupil and teacher were trapped into reacting according to the behavioural and interpretive lenses of their own cultural worlds. And neither seemed able or perhaps willing to peer around the edges of those filters to experiment with different interpretations or behaviours.

Like the teacher and the small boy, people and groups from a common culture tend to act unquestioningly in the range of ways that they have been taught, never thinking to question how these might be experienced or interpreted by those from a different culture. Equally, like the teacher, they will tend to interpret the behaviours and reactions of others according to the lenses of their own habitual assumptions, rarely pausing to wonder whether behaviours or reactions might have a different meaning to the one which they ascribe.

Being the host, and hence the dominant culture in this country, Irish people are probably particularly prone to assume unquestioningly the validity of their accustomed range of behaviours, reactions and interpretations, rarely taking time to explore how these may be experienced by newcomers. This may well have been reinforced in recent years by an increasingly Eurocentric mindset which has at its core values such as time-keeping, efficiency, worth and success. This set of values is profoundly different to the culture and mindsets of many African and Asian ethnic groupings. Because the Eurocentric values tend to reside at a level of sub-consciousness we are only dimly aware of them and hence we tend to act 'as if' they were totally and unquestionably valid.

On the other hand, people coming into Ireland will tend both to act out of and interpret the actions of others according to the assumptive world of their home culture. They may rarely pause either to reflect on or question how their accustomed ways of behaving may be perceived by the majority, or indeed by other ethnic minority groups with whom they now come into contact.

It follows that when individuals or groups from radically differing cultures meet that there is room for misunderstandings and confusion on a grand scale. When members of such diverse groupings come together with the aim of evolving into a transcultural community, albeit on the basis of their shared Christian commitment, it would be optimistic to suggest that the process would be without moments of misunderstanding and complexity.

*Contradictory Culture*

*Three or four families, the core of a small Methodist Church, had become very involved in developing relationships with the thirty or so Congolese and Angolan asylum seekers who had joined the fellowship. They regularly invited the newcomers to their homes, hosted Christmas parties, summer barbeques and embarked on joint outings to the countryside and to historic sites to give a wider sense of Ireland and to create common ground for conversation. In time it appeared that a number of solid new relationships were being built. After a number of years most of the African families were moved out of the hostels where they were initially accommodated and were allocated their own houses by the Department of Social Welfare. As time passed, the Irish group were at first mystified, and then hurt and inclined to withdraw...not one of them had received an invitation to the new homes.*

*What looked like the development of a small but significant impasse was only averted when one family shared their sense of hurt with the African family to whom they were closest. It emerged that the Africans too had been mystified, and indeed somewhat hurt that their new friends had not taken time to visit them in their new homes.*

*The explanation was quite simple: in Congolese or Angolan culture honour is conferred by visiting; it is not deemed to be real friendship if you have to await an invitation. In current, though not necessarily past Irish culture, the honour is conferred through receiving an invitation. It would be considered somewhat impolite to 'invite oneself'. The Irish were waiting to be invited; the Africans were waiting to be visited; meanwhile the beginnings of a divide was emerging, whose source was individuals using their own cultural frame of reference to interpret the actions of others. It did not help that Irish culture and to a lesser extent Congolese and Angolan cultures are all somewhat reticent about actually 'naming' issues; this allowed the impasse to grow.*

*Questioning and exploring rather than assuming the meaning behind a behaviour or range of behaviours, and being conscious of the norms and expectations of a culture, including one's own, is important in multi-cultural engagement.*

*Learning to Live with Cultural Difference*

Cultures are different for a whole variety of reasons having to do with things as diverse as geography, history and climate. Transculturalism promotes the expression and celebration of difference. It encourages groups from different cultures not just to find ways of co-existing but to recognise and be enriched by the diversity of each others' traditions, perceptions and values. This is not as simple as it sounds in the practical business of every day living. Major difficulties can occur when trying to achieve a goal or accomplish a task because different cultures make varying assumptions about how to proceed, the exact nature of the job to be done, and how best to achieve an end result. There are no guaranteed formulae for avoiding such difficulties, however there are a number of useful steps to minimise the difficulties involved.

*Acknowledge and explore difference:* The first major step is to acknowledge that different cultures will have very different ways of thinking and doing. It is worth investing time in getting to know exactly what these differences are and how they affect behaviours, priorities and the definition of goals and roles. Acknowledging and understanding differences is always more productive than fighting them or alternatively ignoring them and becoming frustrated.

*Recognise that no culture has all the answers:* Every culture is inclined to assume that its way of thinking, behaving or prioritising is the correct one. Even if these assumptions are not made explicit, they tend to operate quite powerfully as unquestioned realities at an implicit or unspoken level. Acknowledge that no one culture (even yours!) has the monopoly on the most valid ways of approaching life.

*Recognise your cultural biases:* Recognise that your normal way of doing things, of prioritising, or of reacting probably comes from exposure to your own culture. Appreciate that another culture may have a different way of looking at a task or indeed a completely different way of ranking the priorities.

*Explore your own cultural assumptions:* Become aware of the hidden or semi-hidden range of assumptions which underlie the behaviours, reactions and interpretations of your own cultural group.

*Stand in the others' cultural shoes:* Learn to use your imagination to understand the perspectives and the behaviours of those from another culture.

*Nurture good relationships:* There is nothing to beat open and honest relationships where perceived differences can be acknowledged and explored. Regular discussion of difference, gentle, respectful questioning and an acknowledgement and sharing of any difficulty can all yield positive results. If you don't understand: ask!

In summary, every transcultural congregation needs to put time aside for the following tasks:

- Spend time getting to know about each others cultures, history, traditions.
- Acknowledge together that there may be differences in ways of seeing and doing.
- Examine how these may/will affect behaviours, reactions, interpretations and hence relationships.
- Explore how the different cultures deal with anger and frustration.
- Recognise that cultural difference will tend to affect vision, goals and work pace.
- Imagine together where the difficulties are most likely to arise and for whom.
- Plan how to acknowledge and resolve issues.
- Organise regular occasions where the different cultures can meet, share and discuss.

> *I think there were – and continue to be – three major challenges in developing transcultural congregations. The first is to integrate aspects or styles of worship that are part of new as well as original members' spirituality, thereby allowing everyone to feel at home at some point in the service. I've seen this*

*done in other integrating Churches, through the use of a variety of forms of music, or through spontaneous prayer as well as in other ways; I envy the fact that their leaders have had the insight to enable this to happen. We have done virtually nothing in this regard. The second challenge is to talk and share much more. There are so many things that need to be talked about so that misunderstandings arising from cultural differences do not arise, or can be resolved. We need to provide a forum where things can be discussed. Thirdly there is a challenge to see that new people make the move from "welcome visitors" to members of the congregation. In this respect I got enormous pleasure from overhearing a Cameroonian member welcoming a stranger to the church recently.*

*Micro-cultures and sub-cultures*

Groups who spend time together often begin to behave like – rather large – families. There are many similarities between families and groups, and no two are ever exactly alike. Each has its own micro-culture woven from the interaction of a number significant strands. For instance, every family has a range of explicit *rules* which define the range of behaviours and values that are acceptable as well as an assortment of implicit or unspoken rules and values. While the latter are largely unspoken they can be very powerful. The fact that they are unspoken can often make them all the more difficult to challenge. Both explicit and implicit rules vary radically from household to household and from group to group.

Families also have a variety of explicit *roles*; for instance the roles of father, mother, eldest and youngest sibling, grandparents, cousins, and so on. The function, or what is expected of these roles varies from family to family. For instance, in one, the mother role involves the functions of emotional supporter, housekeeper, financial manager, decision-maker and wage-earner. In another household the mother role may have a lot fewer functions attached, and the father or an older child or a member of the extended family network such as a grandmother may fulfil some of these functions.

Likewise in a Church group or congregation the role of minister may actually include among others the functions of pastor, evangelist, prime decision-maker, administrator and financial controller, while in another congregation the minister is primarily preacher and pastor. Functions relating to administration, decision-making, evangelism and finance are held by other leaders. How a congregation customarily divides up these and other functions, and the personality and vision of those it chooses to fulfil them will feed into the development of a unique local culture as well as dictating what tasks are seen as necessary to be undertaken and how these are accomplished.

There are also implicit roles in every family. The fact that these are often unnamed this does not mean that they are any the less powerful. These include, among others, the carer, who tends to looks after everyone; the stirrer, who always questions; the mascot who represents the family ideal; the scapegoat who is customarily blamed, and the peacekeeper, always striving to smooth things over. Such roles, rarely acknowledged explicitly, are also a part of other human groups. Their existence and the personality of those who occupy them will significantly influence the life and sub-culture of a community or congregation.

Families also have their own individual rituals or ways of doing things; they have the stories they tell about themselves and the boundaries that regulate the ingress or egress of new people or ideas. All these are intimately connected to the prevailing sense of how a group identifies itself.

They are also significant realities in other human groups and together with the perception of its own history all feed into the creation of the subculture of a community or congregation. The resulting 'climate' will tend to define how a group sees itself and how it defines its role in society or wider community. From this will flow the activities in which it engages, the level and quality of participation allowed and the ease with which newcomers are assimilated. For instance, a group or congregation who sees its role as narrowly evangelistic will be unlikely to be involved in primarily political or justice related activities. The culture or climate will also influence how conflict and disagreements are handled; whether they are acknowledged and worked through or ignored and left to fester.

*Eliciting a congregation's sub-cultural map*

*Using observation and question try to uncover the following:*

- *What are the most common stories told about the congregation by members? By outsiders?*
- *Who seems to be most respected in the congregation? Why? What does*

*this reveal about its attitudes and values?*

- *What may the answers to both these questions suggest about the congregations' priorities, dreams, aspirations?*
- *What adjectives are most commonly used by members, and then outsiders, to describe the congregation?(eg warm, staid, enthusiastic, socially aware, strict, open, etc.)*
- *How does the congregation tend to deal with difficulties, disagreements or crises?*
- *What people or behaviours does the congregation consider deviant or unacceptably different? How does it deal with these?*
- *What seem to be the most important rules in the congregation... Explicit?... Implicit?*
- *What rituals or symbols (or lack of them) seem particularly important to this congregation? What may these be saying?*
- *What does the congregation say about its mission and priorities... Explicitly?... Implicitly? Do its activities, buildings, services support this?*

An experience illustrates a number of these elements. A group of new members joined a warm but rather traditionally minded evangelical Church with a strong sense of its Reformed identity. Some of the newcomers were from Africa, others Irish, but originally Catholic. A new minister, himself from overseas and with a rather dominant style of leadership, decided that it would be appropriate to have a large cross on the front of the church building and a lighted candle on the communion table. These suggestions were enthusiastically backed by the new members. The ideas were received, however, with quiet horror by many original members who because of a rather turbulent recent history, tended towards a culture best defined as 'don't rock the boat'. After the initial shock had worn off they reluctantly agreed to the proposal. While they could think of many reasons based in tradition to oppose the suggestions, none of these seemed logical or reasonable enough for open debate without the possibility of serious misunderstanding. The cross and candle went ahead. The discomfort of the older members was never explicitly acknowledged. Instead, it was implicitly expressed through an atmosphere of negativity and quiet unresponsiveness.

Mapping the explicit and implicit rules, roles, the accepted ways of doing things, the attendant rituals and the boundaries, and they will be different in each congregation, will give a clear sense of what changes can be realistically achieved in a particular congregation at a particular time. It will also give some indicators as to how these changes may be best strategised. Deciphering the overall cultural map is important in the process of transcultural development for three reasons.

Firstly, it gives some sense of how a particular congregation will react over time to the range of changes which are central to transcultural development. Some changes can usually be achieved with ease. Others may be much more difficult. Some may be virtually impossible for a particular group at a particular point in time. Using force is the antithesis of transculturaism and may at worst ultimately culminate in the demise of a congregation.

Secondly, knowing and understanding a congregation's cultural map will provide a sense of how best to proceed with a particular programme of development. It will give clear indicators as to what works and how. It will provide information as to how to utilise the strengths and creativity of the group, the gifts of individuals or sub-groups in a way that is positive, productive and inclusive.

Lastly, the internal culture or climate of a congregation usually evolves over years in a largely unconscious process. At a time of change and growth there is an opportunity for the community to become involved in discovering for itself what is really important for them, and to consciously review and perhaps recreate or develop their culture in a new direction. The achievement of such significant change will need to be facilitated and supported through a range of appropriate structures, processes and activities.

## CHANGE

Change is simultaneously exciting and perturbing. Processes of change and development are at the centre of creating transcultural communities. Accustomed ways of doing things shift, novel structures evolve and attitudes broaden to encompass new realities, new possibilities.

> *... transculturalism can appear as a major threat because its about change at all sorts of levels... it implies different ways of worshipping, different*

> *ways of doing things... new experiences of prayer... new ways of being a community. At the beginning it was all very scary... for many people the Church had become a bastion against change rather than a place for steps of faith.*

Change is exciting and energising for many, inviting new possibilities and opening up new horizons. For others it can be very threatening, particularly if it is taking place in areas of life that are central or important to them. (It is no accident that change in religious structure or practice provokes such strong reaction; it does so precisely because this is an area important to many people's sense of identity and security). Hence:

> *So much of what we do in Churches is about preserving our comfort zones and not challenging the status quo.*

It is useful to consider some common reactions to change and to look at some strategies for dealing with the resistance which it can sometimes evoke.

Many people tend to have considerable vested interest in preserving the familiar, if only because it *is* familiar and therefore predictable and safe, even if doesn't work too well. Hence they may fight hard to avoid any disruption to the status quo. This can be true even when the proposed changes seem to be quite in keeping with explicit principles and a named sense of vision. Resistance to change tends to exist at an emotional rather than at a cognitive level and so is not necessarily amenable to logical argument. To complicate matters further, reaction is often sourced at a subconscious level, leaving people unaware of the real source or strength of feelings and out of touch with the degree of resistance which change or challenge can provoke.

Interestingly, resistance to change is not limited to individuals or subgroups. Larger systems or organisations also tend to resist change and can be quite energetic in opposing or sabotaging anything that appears to be a threat to their usual way of being or to their accustomed way of doing things. This can be so even if the the proposed changes would make for a richer or more useful future.

Systems Theory recognises the prevalence and power of this propensity and calls it homeostasis. It suggests that homeostasis is the innate tendency or drive of any individual, system or organisation to mobilise internal and external forces to re-balance itself back towards its accustomed or usual way of functioning, in reaction to the new or innovative. Systems thinkers suggest that such a propensity must be taken very seriously when contemplating or designing for change.

Some important conclusion arise: Firstly, while change is exciting it is also experienced by many as quite threatening and hence needs to be managed carefully and with consideration towards all involved. Secondly, resistance to change is quite normal; it often relates to people's rarely publicised fears and, despite appearances to the contrary, is usually not sourced in pure stubbornness. Thirdly, change and its implications cannot be easily compartmentalised: shift at one level often necessitates change at other levels too. Fourthly, the more important a group or organisation is to an individual, or the more they see themselves as identified with it, the stronger will tend to be their reaction. Lastly, it may not necessarily be the change *per se* that is the issue but people's *perception* of that change and how it may effect them, their roles and their sense of security. Such fears are often quite reasonable; as well as making life more exciting and stimulating for some change will invariably make it much more complicated, uncertain or difficult for others.

Researchers into human behaviour suggest that there are four possible types of change which impinge on those involved in groups or organisations:

- The first is change in the usual structures. This refers to change in areas such as external authority structures or internal organisational arrangements: committee structures, leadership systems and communication networks. It can also include changes in actual physical buildings.
- The second area is policy change: this includes important areas such as a change in mission statement, or in the focus of an organisation's task or reasons for being.
- The third, and the one which will tend to impinge on the largest number of people, is change in accustomed procedures, generally at a local level. In a Church context this may include changes in who is eligible for leadership, the criteria for membership, the establishment and constituency of sub-groups, the definition of their tasks and the

style and conduct of services. Alteration at this procedural level is probably the most visible or noticeable form of change. It is also the one which will tend to attract most reaction.

- The last and probably the most radical form of change is attitudinal; and this may be the slowest and most difficult shift to achieve. Behavioural scientists suggest that change in attitude is not necessarily a *sine qua non* for the other changes to take place: in fact it will often follow and be supported by change first accomplished at other levels. Attitudinal change is also peculiarly susceptible to positive role models, quality of relationship and inclusive leadership styles.

While these four categories are useful, the practical realities of any change process tends to be a lot less neat and watertight. Types of change tend to weave in and out of each other in an untidy and multi-faceted way. All this invites the conclusion that the intensity and indeed the rate of change need to be managed carefully. A key element in this management is an understanding of why people tend to fight shy of the phenomenon. Michael J Hicks a management consultant of international repute puts forward a number of specific reasons as to why people avoid or resist change in the systems of which they are a part. These reasons are very realistic and explain why resistance to change is really quite normal. People are reacting because they are fearful or because they feel everything is shifting too quickly or too radically. It is not necessarily because they are being awkward or cussed. He suggests that negative reaction to change is frequently sourced in the following:

- Fear of the unknown
- Lack of information
- Misinformation
- Historical factors
- Threat to one's core skills and competencies
- Threat to status
- Threat to power base
- Few perceived benefits
- Low trust in the organisational climate
- Poor relationships
- Fear of failure
- Fear of looking stupid

- Reluctance to experiment
- Bound to closely to tradition and custom
- Reluctance to let go

These reactions are very real; they often constitute very reasonable responses to possible change so it is important to recognise them and attend to them. As a result change needs to be managed carefully. Too much change too soon, or without adequate information may cause a counter reaction and reversal. Too little and nothing happens at all and the status quo remains virtually unaltered.

*There will often be people who have had a lot of influence in running the Church for years. In small congregations you're often very dependant on individuals who have worked exceptionally hard for years to make the Church viable or indeed to keep it open and they can end up holding a lot of influence or indeed power. While such a level of commitment can be necessary to keep the doors open it is not always a good thing, because it entails those involved putting so much energy into the Church that they have little time for other interests and commitments and they become personally over identified with their role in the congregation. Of course its important to remember that this has been allowed to happen because it suited everyone else to let them get on with it… and this includes the Church authorities at both a local and Diocesan level. You can, not infrequently, end up with a situation where the only place that such a person now has influence or a meaningful role is in the Church. And of course when change happens they can become very threatened and resistant to anything that may disrupt this. If they are not flexible, or are very set in their way of doing things or are really wedded to holding onto their influence or power this can be a huge difficulty. Hence transculturalism can appear as a major threat because it's about change at all sorts of levels; it implies quite profound change in a Church. It can take time and the wisdom of Solomon to help people to let go, or to move over, or to engage in other ways of expressing themselves or of finding validation.*

The action of developing transcultural communities involves constant change as people cope with finding new ways of doing things, develop new ways of relating to each other and learn to question old modes of behaviour. There are a number of useful ways of attending to the disturbance which such change can create. Thomas Cummings and Christopher Worley [3] in a recent book on change in organisations invite attention to three of these:

*Empathic Listening:* Firstly there needs to be a concern to listen to how people are experiencing the changes. The emphasis here is not just on hearing what people are saying but on eliciting what they may be *feeling.* This process will not only identify those who are having difficulty; it will also provide useful information about a wide range of issues related to the project. Moreover, when people are listened to carefully and non-judgementally, with a genuine concern to understand their views and feelings, they will tend to be much less defensive and much more willing to engage in constructive resolution of the issue to hand and more generally in an active ownership of the project.

*Effective Communication:* Secondly, people become restive, uncertain and hence resentful if they do not know what is happening. Rumour takes over and fears become rampant. Setting up clear channels of two-way communication, as well as honouring and utilising existing informal ones, is vital. These need to ensure that those involved understand what is happening or what is planned and have a clear method of feeding their views and questions back into the process.

*Inclusion and Participation:* Thirdly, people often resist because they feel excluded or out of control. One of the most efficient ways to overcome this difficulty is to involve members directly and from the outset in planning and envisioning for change. This not only provides a greater range of new ideas and perspectives it also involves people in the ownership and moulding of a shared purpose.

What is being advocated here is a shift from a 'top down' method of instituting change to a 'bottom up' approach, which privileges *consultation, transparency* and *participation.* This demands a transformation in the mindset of many leaders, from one which directs, to one which enters into co-operative engagement and dialogue. Traditionally, Churches of virtually all denominational backgrounds have tended to adhere to a very directive and hierarchical model of decision-making at both local and institutional levels. Consultation and participative management have

3. T. Cummings and C. Worley, *Organisation, Development and Change,* 2005, London: Thomson.

been honoured more in the breach than the observance. Leadership styles have often been authoritarian, if not autocratic, and decision making processes closed to scrutiny and review.

Developments in the theory and practice of organisational management emphasise that while these leadership attributes may have worked in the past they are not suited to the rapidly changing environment of the present. Community development theorists suggest that authoritarian and non-participative leadership and decision-making styles result in impoverished decision-making, disempowered communities and an alienated grass-roots. Both groups advocate the creation of institutional structures which privilege dialogue, participation and transparency as the most effectual and useful way for organisations to develop efficiently, ethically and productively. This fits with the core of transcultural development.

Central to this alternative position is a way of being rather than a set of tools or strategies. It underlines, instead, the importance of respectful engagement with as many individuals and subgroups of those involved as possible. It privileges consultation, feedback and a respect for difference which facilitates the emergence of a joint vision. It emphasises the importance of an ongoing review of decision making processes to insure their transparency. Working *with* a community to nurture the emergence of an inclusive picture of their future creates a climate of participation. This in turn minimises the threat element of transformation as it gives people information and a sense of control over the rate and agenda of change. It also tends to create a far more inclusive end product, incorporating the views, opinions and life experience of many people and a far richer process of development. Such a process will tend to reduce the disturbing elements of the changes, as those from many different backgrounds learn to relate, disagree and problem solve in a mutually enriching process, co-creating multiculturalism as they go.

## LEARNING

Engaging in new learning seems to be an important part of the process of adaptation when a refugee or asylum-seeker begins to connect with their new environment. Sahr Yambasu was head of a theological college in his native Sierra Leone; when he came to Ireland the only employment he could find at first was as a part-time worker in an abattoir. He describes the central moment of transformative learning which occurred for him. Finding himself in a new and alien culture, he re-evaluated his view of himself and his circumstances. This moment of insight led to a profound change that allowed him to connect positively with the challenges of the new context:

> It was the dawn of a new day of seeing and being. While I had experienced a physical border crossing, I was now on the verge of crossing another border...It ushered in a profound rethink on my circumstances.[4]

Radical educational theorists take the view that real learning is about entering a process which facilitates change in assumptions, prejudices and values. This in turn allows for the emergence of new ways of seeing, thinking and behaving. The crises experiences of life, or its times of challenge and difficulty, are seen as contexts in which much qualitative learning can take place.

The displacement which is at the core of the experience of becoming a refugee is one such context. It can result in moments of re-evaluation and growth.

Involvement in the co-construction of transcultural communities is less dramatic but, with its emphasis on creating real connection with those of radically different cultures, it often invites similar times of reflection and re-evaluation. Those involved will constantly find themselves catapulted into new or challenging experiences as they engage with others of different culture. Differences of expectation, misunderstanding of intention or behaviour and a challenge to one's accepted ways of seeing the world are all part of the picture.

Jack Mezirow, a leading theorist in Adult and Continuing Education, agrees that real learning involves more than the development of new sets of skills. At a much deeper level it calls on us to confront and question the assumptions and expectations which underlie our usual attitudes and behaviours. The new responses that are called for imply not

4. S. Yambasu, 'Interrogating Displacement' in A. Ryan A. and T. Walsh (eds.) *Frightening the Horses* , 2004, Maynooth: MACE, p. 38.

5. J. Mezirow, *Transformative Dimensions of Adult Learning*, 1991, San Fransisco: Jossey Bass.

just the development of different ways of doing but different ways of thinking. They demand the deconstruction and re-making of pre-existing meaning systems as well as a revision of our usual ways of doing and being.

An Irish congregation moving from the position of 'doing for' to 'doing with' is one such example. It implies a huge shift in attitude, a letting go both of power, and a change in a familiar way of responding: this allows for the development of a new range of skills and behaviours:

> *Looking back at the transcultural developments in the Church, I suspect that one of the most significant, and one of the hardest things to do is to shift the mindset from 'doing for' to 'doing with' or indeed 'being with'. Doing for the other has become an accepted way in Western Christianity, it's the old charity model that assumes that I have the sweeties and that I can just give them to you because you've nothing. Its much more comfortable, because that way I can preserve the status quo, I don't have to get too close or too involved and of course that means that I retain the upper hand. It implies that you need my largesse, rather than recognising that while you may not have certain resources at present you have many, many others. Its much, much easier to give money or even to develop a support scheme of some kind, than to work with or explore what we can develop together. We did a lot of the former at the beginning and of course some of it may be necessary at the start but you must move because otherwise it creates huge dependency and fosters low self esteem. 'Doing for' doesn't honour the personhood of the other in the same way that entering into a relationship or working out the complexities of developing a co-operative project does. Its much, much harder to open your heart or open your home than it is to open your pocket.*

Transcultural development does not demand such radical shifts in every situation. Sometimes it is quite possible to take familiar skills or ways of seeing, believing and doing, and by extending these, or by building on their foundation, to develop a new range of responses, which will fit the new realities. Sometimes the demands are just too great, too much to contemplate and people retrench. A number of those interviewed noted the fear that is often experienced as members, leaders or ministers feel the safe and familiar slipping from their grasp. They commented on the rationalisations or control mechanisms exercised in order to keep the unknown at bay.

The threat involved in new learning can be just too much and it becomes easier to ignore the demands of the new, to deny the necessity for change. The temptation then is to become busied with reassuring activities or to re-invest in behaviours and positions which reinforce a sense of personal or organisational power and control.

People interviewed also commented on the profound courage of many as they engage with the challenge of the new, as they enter the exciting waters of creating new ways of seeing and doing and making sense of the world. New learning can be very threatening, particularly when it involves not just 'doing' differently, but 'being' differently: there is something very unsettling for most of us in confronting our prejudices and our assumptions. Neither the traditional educational system nor the Churches – nor, indeed society at large – have been particularly enthusiastic about promoting this level of reflection and learning. As a result, it is often difficult for individuals or groups to know quite how to engage in these new levels of learning.

Leading writers on adult learning theory advance some useful guidelines here. D. Boud[6] suggests that a key to new learning which results in change is to engage in reflection. In his thinking this reflective practice has three stages for those engaged in learning.

Firstly, focus on significant life events or experiences, noticing your feelings, senses and observations;

Secondly, explore the wider ideological, organisational or cultural contexts of which these events or experiences are a part and note how the wider systems influence you. Notice too how your feelings influence your attitude to and handling of the systems.

Thirdly, consider how you could take the initiative, to intervene and create change in these wider contexts

Stephen Brookfield[7] proposes a similar model, suggesting that the process of critical reflection lies at the heart of learning and consequent change. He suggests that in the process of critical reflection, one's as-

6. D. Boud, R. Keogh and D. Walker (eds.), *Reflection: Turning Experiences into Learning*, 1989, London: Kogan Page.

7. S. Brookfield, *Developing Critical Thinkers*, 1987, San Fransisco: Jossey-Bass.

sumptions and presuppositions are first of all made conscious and then assessed for their appropriateness, accuracy or fit. When our underlying meaning schemes are made consciously explicit they no longer have the same power to control our thinking and can be changed in a conscious and rational way.

The idea of critical reflection can become a useful tool with which members of different groupings, or indeed any group or individual, can engage in an acknowledgement, exploration and critique of their own assumptive worlds and of the assumptions of the worlds and structures which they inhabit. This means that they 'go after' the maps of their automatic interpretations and reactions and allow them to emerge into consciousness. This allows individuals or groups to become aware of the frames of reference, meaning systems and presuppositions which they automatically employ to order and live life. Being aware of these does not necessarily mean having to change them; it does, however, provide an alertness as to why we may react in a certain mode in particular situations. This in turn allows the possibility of owning such reactions and of explaining them to others. It also allows them to be changed or modified if this seems appropriate.

Critical reflection also means interrogating the systems and organisations that are relevant, looking behind the façade, examining agendas, communication patterns, vision and mission statements. It means critiquing activities to see whether they are actually translating the values which they espouse into their everyday way of being in the world. It means exploring how they handle, use or abuse power.

This process was at the heart of the learning engaged in by a number of those interviewed:

> *What has shocked me is not the challenges encountered but my reactions, of being intolerant, of trying to maintain control ... This has been very challenging for me personally; ministers are very invested in maintaining control. Some of it comes from the training and maybe some is due to the personality types that are selected for ministry. I have had to put a lot of work into learning to be more open, more flexible; to shifting my comfort levels, to let go of control.*

This quotation instances the use of reflection, focusing on the honest appraisal of a personal experience, and using the process to create profound change in the individual's way of being.

> *Reflective process exercise*
> *Take a significant meeting/service/activity and ask the following questions of it:*
> *Why do we as a congregation conduct in this particular way?*
> *Whose reality or usual way of doing things does it privilege?*
> *Who benefits form things remaining as they are?*
> *Who does it include? Exclude?*
> *How may it appear to those of another culture?*
> *What meanings, values or cultural assumptions are embedded in it?*
> *What would have to change for it to become more inclusive? More participative?*
> *How could it become more meaningful for those of other cultures?*
> *Have they been consulted? Are they involved?*

Another respondent used a reflective process to acknowledge and analyse the feelings of frustration he was experiencing in his situation. After some reflection, he contextualised these feelings as a reaction to dynamics within the local Church system as it reacted against the changes inherent in transcultural development. This led him to a re-assessment and critique of the normal and accustomed modes of decision making in the denomination and to locate the local reactions as being related to the conservative agenda of the wider Church. It also alerted him to a fresh realisation of the power of the wider society's ideology to influence the systems within it, including the Church.

Such insights and the accompanying questioning attitude indicate an ability to acknowledge, analyse and critique which is core to new learning. It is about learning to see things as they are.

> *So many of our committees, rituals, offices and assemblies are about preserving the power and status of the denominational structure, or the elders or the clergy or the self, rather than about trying to follow Jesus effectively. Most particularly much of it is about preserving a very eurocentric value system which privileges individuality, success and certainty.*

*Questions to promote Critical Reflection*
*Why am I interpreting this person's behaviour in only this way?*
*What might a more useful/positive/freeing interpretation?*
*Why do I/we experience a strong reaction to a certain behaviour/event?*
*Where do my/our reactions come from?*
*Did they come from my/our expectations/wants being unmet?*
*Were these expectations/wants reasonable? Useful?*
*Had I/we made these clear to the others involved?*
*What could I/we have done differently?*
*How might the other person/group have interpreted my/our expectations?*
*How can I/we involve the other individual/group in learning from this?*

*Because we're so used to the assumptions that are involved we're inclined to accept things as they are without any real question. In fact things are 'as they are' because our society or our Church has chosen to construct its world and its priorities in a particular way. We need to be aware that there are always choices, always different ways of doing things or seeing things. Real intercultural engagement challenges us to realise that there are so many different ways of viewing reality, of prioritising, of doing things differently.*

The learning journey which is at the core of transcultural development calls on participants to extend their existing range of mind sets, responses and behaviours in order to fit with new experiences. At its centre however there is also a much deeper and more radical invitation which implies a questioning of the assumptions which lie at the base of both familiar culture and personal attitudes and reactions. Once this quite radical position has been assumed, it in turn tends to nurture a way of being in the world which is much less willing to allow the status quo of Church or state to go unchallenged and uncritiqued.

## CONCLUSION

The development of transcultural community implies meaningful engagement between those whose life, experience, and ways of seeing and doing may be profoundly different. An understanding of the implications of cultural difference will be useful in highlighting or exploring areas of potential difficulty and as a basis for developing greater understanding. Those involved in transcultural engagement are involved in a journey which explores culture, encounters change and engages with new ventures in transformative learning. If this transaction is real, something core to individual and to group identity is changed. The world and the self can no longer be viewed as in the past.

Transculturalism, as defined by Anne Ryan[8] is a mode of connection or community which demands a meeting on equal terms. It honours equality, inclusivity and participation. It is a distinctive way of connecting, a way as Alan Martin points out, honoured by the New Testament Church.[9] At the core of transcultural engagement is an encounter with the other which seeks neither to change nor to judge, but to share and understand, to truly meet and learn of the other and to create the structures that will furnish the continuance of this process. To really meet the other is always to be changed at some deep level.

The process of transculturalism invites critical reflection not just on the individuals and congregations involved and their realities. It will also invite attention to anomalies, abuses and inequalities which are central to society and indeed to the Churches' ways of functioning. It remains to be seen whether these structures will respond appropriately.

*Despite the very real challenges developing a transcultural congregation was, and continues to be a most profoundly rewarding pathway; really quite wonderfully enriching for the Church and for the individuals and families involved – although certainly a steep learning curve.*

8. See 'Levels of Engagement between Cultures', pp. 15-23, *supra*.
9. See 'The Ephesian Moment', pp. 24-77, *supra*.